AF477977

Changing Rules of Delegation

Changing Rules of Delegation

A Contest For Power in Comitology

By Adrienne Héritier, Catherine Moury,
Carina Bischoff, and Carl Fredrik Bergström

OXFORD
UNIVERSITY PRESS

OXFORD
UNIVERSITY PRESS

Great Clarendon Street, Oxford, OX2 6DP,
United Kingdom

Oxford University Press is a department of the University of Oxford.
It furthers the University's objective of excellence in research, scholarship,
and education by publishing worldwide. Oxford is a registered trade mark of
Oxford University Press in the UK and in certain other countries

First Edition published in 2013

Impression: 1

British Library Cataloguing in Publication Data

Data available

Library of Congress Cataloging in Publication Data

Data available

ISBN 978-0-19-965362-1

Printed in Great Britain by
MPG Books Group, Bodmin and King's Lynn

Outline Contents

Table of contents

List of Tables

Introduction

With each legislative issue on the agenda, legislators have to decide whether to delegate decision-making power to the executive and/or to expert decision-making bodies in order to flesh out the details of this legislation, or, alternatively, to spell out all aspects of this decision in legislation proper. The reasons guiding the choice for delegation have been of prime interest to political science for a long time. The theoretical debate has concentrated on principal–agent theory to explain why and how politicians delegate decision making to bureaucrats, to independent regulatory agencies, and to other actors and how to control these agents (Strom 2000; Majone 1996; Lupia and McCubbins 2000; Pollack 2003; McCubbins and Schwartz 1984). By contrast, our research focuses on the questions: Which actors are empowered by the choice for delegation? Are executive actors empowered over legislative actors? And how do legislative actors react to the loss of empowerment? What opportunities are there for legislative actors to change the institutional rules governing delegation to executive decision making in order to (re)gain institutional power, and with it influence over policy outcomes? And, finally, do actors adjust their behaviour to the changes of a delegation rule, and if yes, how?

We analyse the conditions and processes of the changing of rules that delegate decision-making powers to the Commission's implementing powers under comitology. We focus on the role of the European Parliament (the Parliament) in this process of delegation and use institutionalist, power-based bargaining theory in order to account for why the Commission, the Council, and increasingly the Parliament did or did not choose to delegate decision making to the Commission. If they chose delegation, they still had to determine under which institutional rule comitology should operate. These rules, too, distribute power unequally among actors and therefore raise the question of how they came about in the first place, and whether and how the 'losers' of a rule change at t1 seek to alter the rules at a later point in time *t2*.

Our theoretical argument is based on the assumptions that boundedly rational actors will seek to maximize their institutional power in order to increase their influence over outcomes. Given bounded rationality and transaction costs, negotiated rules constitute incomplete contracts. Building on J. Knight's (1992) distributive bargaining theory we expect that the preferences of actors regarding the choice of delegation will depend on their competences under delegation. Accordingly, a change in the procedures governing delegation which implies a shift in competences between actors will induce a change in the preferences for delegation. The actor who gained competences under delegation will increasingly choose to delegate, whereas the actor who suffered a relative loss in competences will not choose to delegate. These assumptions also lead us to conjecture that those losing out under a specific institutional rule will seek to renegotiate in the course of its application in order to change it in their own favour.

We focus on the question of how the Parliament over time has asserted its role under delegation. In the early years of delegated legislation the Parliament was all but absent in the system of delegated legislation. Under the Lisbon Treaty it has become a co-equal partner with the Council of Ministers under the 'Delegated Acts' of Art. 290. How did this astounding change of institutional rules come about? By which means did the Parliament obtain these new competences under the Lisbon Treaty and what do they imply for the present and future of delegated legislation in the EU? We show how the Parliament step by step wrenched power from the Council and the Commission until it became an equal partner of the Council under 'Delegated Acts' (Art. 290) of the Lisbon Treaty. It achieved this aim by systematically blocking decision-making processes in other decision-making arenas under co-decision and the budgetary process, using this lever to force the Council to yield formal powers to the Parliament under comitology (see Chapter 3).

Using quantitative statistical analysis we then show how important is delegated legislation in the context of legislative activity in the EU. We demonstrate that we are focusing on a large bulk of decision making and not on some marginal phenomenon of European legislation. More specifically, of all regulations and directives between 1970 and 2006, 22.8 per cent constituted legislation and 77.2 per cent was delegation. Of the regulations and directives in force in 2008, 25.9 per cent was legislation and 74.1 per cent was delegation (see Chapter 4). What emerges from a further quantitative analysis focused on environmental policy is that the Parliament—although disempowered by delegation under co-decision—does not oppose delegation altogether, yet systematically restricts the substantive scope of individual delegation items in order to protect its co-legislative powers under co-decision (see Chapter 5). And—looking exclusively at the Commission's and the Council's preferences regarding delegation and legislation—we examine the consequences of a rule change empowering the Commission over the Council.

The book is organized as follows: The first chapter offers some background information on the Commission's implementing powers and the comitology system. In the second, theoretical, chapter we briefly summarize the literature on why actors choose to delegate in the first place, summarizing the arguments of political science principal–agent theory. We then turn to the theoretical foundation of our research question of why the rules governing delegation under comitology changed over time and develop our institutionalist power-based bargaining argument. Based on the assumptions that actors tend to choose the institutional rule that maximizes their institutional power, and hence their influence over policy outcomes, and assuming that institutions are incomplete contracts, we hypothesize that actors disadvantaged by an existing rule will seek to renegotiate it in order to increase their power. This renegotiation may occur across arenas, with decisions in one arena held hostage in order to achieve a desired outcome in another arena. In the empirical part of the book, the third and fourth chapters present a longitudinal qualitative analysis to empirically assess the theoretically derived hypotheses on institutional change. We show how the Commission, the Council, and increasingly the Parliament negotiated (and are still negotiating) decision-making power in the comitology system; why and how these rules changed; and how they in turn triggered attempts by the 'losers' to alter them to their own benefit. In the quantitative empirical part of the book, the fifth chapter gives a statistical overview of the number and areas of legislation and delegation respectively, and shows how comitology decisions developed over time and according to policy areas. In the sixth and seventh chapters we quantitatively test a batch of our hypotheses by presenting and analysing data on delegation and non-delegation; legislation in environmental policy (Chapter 6); and taxation and agricultural policy (Chapter 7). Chapter 8 concludes by discussing findings in the light of our theoretically derived hypotheses and considers the practical implications of the change of rules governing comitology today.

1

European legislation and comitology: The development of the comitology system

The comitology system dates back to the 1960s, when the Council, overburdened with implementation of the common agricultural policy (CAP), decided to delegate some of its implementing powers to the Commission (Bergström 2005). However, a majority of member states still wanted to retain some control over the Commission, hence committees of member states were set up to supervise the Commission's implementing activities—the so-called 'comitology committees'. These committees have been engaged in two functions in delegated legislation: cooperation and coordination at a preparatory stage; and control at the stage of formal decision making.

While the legality of these committees was confirmed in 1970 by the European Court of Justice, it was only at the end of the 1980s that they became formally defined and recognized. The Single European Act clearly identified the right to confer implementing powers as a prerogative of the Council. It also provided the latter with explicit authority to lay down the conditions under which the Commission exercises its delegated authority. However, in contrast to the legislative procedure, the Treaty did not specify the procedures of delegation to be used in a particular policy area, and it reserved a primary role for the Council in determining the procedures that should be applied in a given instance (Bergström 2005).

The First Council Comitology Decision, in 1987, featured three types of committees that member states could choose to use on the basis of a draft from the Commission: advisory committees whose vote was not binding on the Commission; management committees in which—in case of disagreement with the proposed Commission implementing a measure—the Commission had to forward the measure to the Council; and regulatory committees in which the Commission's draft decisions had to be approved by a decision supported by a qualified majority of the votes cast in the Council (QMV). Hence, while in the case of management committees the Commission needed only to avoid having a qualified majority of member states against its draft, in the case of regulatory committees it needed a qualified majority expressly supporting it.

Moreover, the 1987 Comitology Decision, against the explicit wish of the Commission (and the EP), also provided for two variants of the management and regulatory committees. When a management committee disagreed with a Commission's draft, under the first procedure the Commission could enact the measure with the Council having one month to annul or modify it by QMV; under the second procedure the Commission had to defer the measure for three months, after which it was adopted unless the Council rejected or modified it by QMV. There were also two variants of the regulatory committee: one with a 'net', under which the Council could reject the measure by QMV; and one with a 'safety net', under which the Council was able to reject the measure by a simple majority. In both cases, however, the Council needed unanimity to modify the proposed measure; if the Council could not reach a decision within a certain period of time, the Commission could proceed as originally planned. Finally, the 1987 Council decision also provided for a more exceptional 'safeguard procedure', to be used when the Commission had been granted powers to adopt temporary safeguard procedures; it also recalled that the Council could delegate implementing powers to itself rather than to the Commission.

This decision was in force for more than a decade until it was changed in 1999, mainly in order to address the Parliament's concerns about being excluded from the comitology system. Parliament's apprehensions were all the more compelling, since with the Maastricht Treaty the Parliament had become a co-legislator under co-decision making. The new Council decision introduced three innovations. First, it abolished the second variant of both the management and regulatory procedures. Second, it included criteria to guide the choice of specific comitology procedures. The management committee was to be used for the implementation of the common agricultural and fisheries policies, and more generally for programmes with substantial budgetary implications. The regulatory procedure was to be used to apply essential provision of basic instruments or to update non-essential elements of a legislative act. The advisory committee procedure was to be used for the remaining cases. However, the Council also provided that these criteria were of a non-binding nature—a provision which was subsequently confirmed by the European Court of Justice. Finally, the new decision included various mechanisms to inform the Parliament of the comitology committees' activities (Bergström 2005).

Table 1.1 Main changes included in the 1999 Comitology Decision for the three most frequently used committees

Committee	1987 Council Decision	1999 Comitology Decision	2006 Comitology Decision
Advisory	The Commission must take the 'utmost account of the committee's opinion'	No change	No change
Management	The Commission may enact the measure unless the committees oppose it by QMV, if not:	No change	No change
	A: the Commission may enact the measure but the Council has one month to take a different decision by QMV	3 months rather than 1 month	No change
	B: the Commission must defer the measure for three months. The measure will be enacted unless the Council takes a different decision by QMV	Abolished	No change
Regulatory	The Commission may only enact the measure when the committee agrees by QMV, if not:	No change	No change
	'Net': the Commission adopts the measure if the Council has not acted (by QMV) within three months	Added: right of information of the EP Added: if the Council opposes the proposal, the Commission must re-examine it and may resubmit an amended proposal or a legislative proposal.	
	'Safety Net': the Commission adopts the measure if the Council has not acted (by QMV) within three months *and if the council has not rejected the measure by simple majority*	Abolished	
			'Regulatory with scrutiny': EP and Council have the ability to block the adoption of the proposed measure and the Commission has to present a new draft measure or a new proposal for legislation

The Second Comitology Decision was revised in 2006. It created a new regulatory procedure ('regulatory procedure with scrutiny') to be used for acts adopted under co-decision. Under this procedure the Commission had to submit its draft implementation measure to the regulatory committee and to both the Council and the Parliament, even after it had received a positive opinion from the committee. Both the Council and the Parliament were able to block the adoption of the proposed measure and send the proposal back to the committee. If it was rejected, the Commission would have to present a new draft measure or a new proposal for legislation (Bergström 2005: 249–85; Bergström and Héritier 2007; Bergström et al. 2007; Ponzano 2009).[1]

The Treaty of Lisbon broke new ground by distinguishing for the first time between legislative delegation and executive delegation. Accordingly, it established two separate procedures for 'Delegated Acts' and implementing acts. Under 'Delegated Acts' the Commission—by legislation—may be delegated the power to adopt acts supplementing or amending certain non-essential elements of the legislation in question. Both the Council and the Parliament may prevent 'Delegated Acts' from entering into force within a certain period of time. Under implementing acts the Commission—by legislation—may be delegated the power to give detail to legislation that needs to be uniformly implemented across member states, under the control of the member states (comitology) (Ponzano 2010). In order to distinguish the 'Delegated Acts' under Art. 290 of the Treaty on the Functioning of the European Union (TFEU) from the political science term of delegated decision making to executive bodies in a general sense, inverted commas are used throughout the text when referring to 'Delegated Acts' under Art. 290 TFEU.

In December 2010, a new comitology regulation was adopted by co-decision. It replaced the old management and regulatory procedures with an examination procedure, in which the Council no longer functions as body of appeal in cases of conflict. The new regulation also includes a right of scrutiny for the co-legislators. The Parliament and the Council can alert the Commission whenever they consider that a draft implementation act exceeds the implementing powers provided for in the basic legal act. The Parliament, Council, and the Commission also agreed on a Common Understanding on 'Delegated Acts', in which the Commission commits itself to consult with member states when preparing a 'delegated act'.

---

[1] Comitology Decision 2006/512/EC

2

Theory and hypotheses

2.1 Why delegate and how to control the agent

When studying the delegation of implementing powers to the Commission the first question that arises is the 'why' of delegation. A vast body of political science literature using principal–agent theory deals with this question and with the conditions of delegation to the executive, to committees, and to independent regulatory authorities. In particular, this body of research includes literature on the US Congress delegating tasks to bureaucracy on the one side, and the literature on regulation and independent regulatory authorities on the other. A number of studies have also applied principal–agent theory to the delegation of implementing powers to the Commission, addressing the questions of the 'why' and 'how' of delegation to comitology (Pollack 1997, 2003; Epstein and O'Halloran 1999b; Franchino 2002, 2004, 2007).

This literature offers answers as to the motives of delegation and as to how the principal—while delegating—still seeks to ensure that the agent does not overstretch his mandate. While the focus of this book rests on the question of why under comitology actors prefer one institutional rule governing delegation over another, and how these institutional rules change over time, it is necessary to at least briefly summarize the principal–agent theory on the why and how of delegation. One reason is that it constitutes the 'classic' theoretical literature on delegation and beyond; the 'why of delegation' also raises the question of how the principal may succeed in controlling the agent by using specific rules governing delegation. These institutional rules governing comitology and their change with regard to the role of the EP, and not the motives of delegation, are at the heart of our study. The other reason is that—in order to analyse the willingness of actors to delegate under specific rules—we need to control factors which might increase the likelihood of the actors to delegate, such as the number of member states and the policy areas in which delegation occurs. These are important questions raised by principal–agent theory when discussing the 'why' of delegation on which we therefore offer some background knowledge.

Principal–agent theory, as applied in political science,[1] has developed the motives and mechanisms of delegation between a principal and an agent in which the agent acts on behalf of the principal in a particular domain of decision making (Ross 1973: 134). It assumes that the agent has more information than the principal, one important reason for delegating in the first place, and it further assumes that the agent takes actions that impact upon the pay-offs of both, the principal and the agent. The principal has the formal authority to impose incentives on the agent. He/she will use these incentives in order to compensate for any informational disadvantage (Miller 2005: 204). By shaping the agent's incentives, the principal seeks to reduce the likelihood that the agent will not act in accordance with the principal's preferences. For the agent—while following the wishes of the principal—may also pursue his/her own objectives.

When applying principal–agent theory to comitology it is assumed that the relationship between the Council and the Commission's implementing powers may be conceived of as a relationship of *delegation,* i.e. the Council charges the Commission with the task of fleshing out primary legislation. In this task the agent/Commission acquires a great deal of expertise and develops an informational advantage vis-à-vis the member governments/principals. If the latter fail to develop means of taming the agent, the very purpose of comitology procedures, which allow for a mechanism of control and active participation of member

---

[1] Normative economic principal–agent theory focuses on the voluntary contract between two parties which establishes a collaborative relationship in order to come to a mutually profitable exchange. Economic principal–agent theory (most prominently Arrow 1985; Akerlof 1970; Ross 1973; Laffont and Tirole 1993) starts from the assumption of perfect rationality and complete information and focus on the causes and effects of conflicting incentives and asymmetric information in the application of a contract. It proposes to define ex ante the contract in such a way as to offer incentives for the agent and the principal to reduce the risks of cooperation and to comply with the contract, i.e. adverse selection (to choose the wrong agent) and with 'moral hazard' (non-compliance with the contractual obligations). The underlying notion is that of a complete contract. Thus, the question of what happens after delegation is not raised by normative economic principal–agent theory; the possible developments are anticipated and included in the devising of the contract by formulating the right incentives for agent and principal—negative developments are to be pre-empted (Karagiannis 2007: 24). By contrast, political science principal–agent theory as applied to the delegation relationships between political actors and bureaucracy, and political actors and regulatory authorities, has mostly based its arguments on the assumption of bounded rationality and incomplete contracts and asks how the principal seeks to maintain his control over the agent in the post-contract phase.

governments in the task of adding detail to legislation by issuing decisions on how to implement legislation jointly with the Commission,[2] is undermined.

In the following section we first briefly outline the main arguments for the 'why' of delegation discussed in the principal–agent literature, then turn to the question of 'how to control the agent', i.e. the developing of institutional rules governing delegation.

2.1.1 *Why delegate?*

Why—in view of the risk of agency shirking (i.e. behaviour that deviates from the objective of the original delegation)—would principals decide to delegate decision making to an agent? The causes and political motives behind the act of delegation (McCubbins 1985: 721) have been extensively discussed in the literature, the most frequently mentioned motivation being substantive uncertainty and the need for expertise; political uncertainty; policy credibility; and blame shifting.[3]

Substantive policy uncertainty and the need for expertise as reasons for delegation in politics were already emphasized by Max Weber as a prime motive for delegation of decision making to expert public bodies that are separate from the main avenue of legitimate representative government (Weber 1958, cited in Miller 2005).[4] Principal–agent theory starts out from the assumption that the agent through his/her policy expertise has an informational advantage over the principal and that he/she takes actions that impact upon both the principal and him/herself (Fiorina 1982, 1986; McCubbins 1985; McCubbins et al. 1987; Horn and Shepsle 1989; Pollack 2003; Miller 2005). Discerning between different degrees of uncertainty and demand for expertise of various policy areas, the principal–agent literature on delegation to comitology has distinguished between complex and non-complex areas and found

---

[2] Traditionally a distinction is made between 'primary' and 'secondary' legislation. The essential difference between the two is in the level at which the authorization for adopting an act is found. The category 'primary' legislation denotes that an act has been adopted directly on the basis of a provision in the Treaty. The category 'secondary' legislation, by contrast, denotes that an act has been adopted on the basis of a provision in a pre-existing piece of 'primary' legislation, and therefore only indirectly on the basis of a provision of the Treaty. Another way of putting this is that secondary legislation is the result of a delegation of powers originating in the Treaty. For present purposes the notion 'legislation' will be used in a more narrow sense, to denote only primary legislation. The term 'delegation' will be used to denote secondary legislation, thus emphasizing the conditional nature of the power exercised.

[3] For a systematic, theoretical, and empirical discussion of the question of the extent of independence of agents from their principals in the field of competition policy, see Guidi (2010).

[4] Quoted in Miller 2005: 203.

evidence that complex policy areas requiring expertise are more likely to be subject to comitology (Epstein and O'Halloran 1999; Franchino 2002, 2004, 2007; Pollack 2003).

If substantive policy uncertainty and the need for expertise is one important cause for the delegation of policymaking to comitology, political uncertainty is another. Political uncertainty appears and is discussed in two quite different forms: (i) to ensure policy stability over time; (ii) to ensure that a policy decision is taken in the first place. The first cause (i) refers to the wish of governments to protect their policy choices from being dismantled by their successor governments (Moe 1990).[5] This argument of political uncertainty is closely related to the 'credible commitment' argument developed by Majone (1996). He argues that delegation to independent regulatory authorities responds to a need for policy stability in the regulation of the economy and seeks to ensure that after a change in government these policies—important for private economic actors' investment decisions—are not dismantled (Majone 1996: 1).

A different (ii) form of political uncertainty argument was presented by Fiorina (1982), who argued that interest groups with diverse preferences might mutually block each other in the legislative process and might therefore be unable to come to an agreement supporting detailed legislation. In order to avoid stalled decision making, legislators linked with different interest groups will agree that authority be delegated to agents/bureaucracy/agencies with the task to take detailed decisions, while legislation takes only the form of a (relatively) vague mandate or framework legislation. Mere framework legislation may be agreed upon much more easily than a specific mandate, and may save the transaction costs of information gathering and bargaining among political actors with diverse preferences; thereby it offers a possible escape route out of a threatening decision-making impasse.[6] Using this argument in the context of European legislation it could be argued that member governments with diverse preferences will seek to avoid costly efforts to reach political agreement in the legislative process and will therefore decide to delegate responsibility for legislative details to the Commission's implementing powers. In a similar argument and referring to the institutional structure in which the legislative process of a polity is embedded, Epstein and O'Halloran (1999)—assuming divergence of preferences of the

---

[5] See also Gilardi, who measures political uncertainty as the replacement risk of a government with preferences A by a government with preferences B and the likelihood that political actors will delegate decisions to independent regulatory authorities (Gilardi 2005).

[6] For the European Union, see Héritier 1999.

formal players—argue that in more cohesive legislatures with few veto players, legislators tend to delegate less because the details of the policy can be more easily agreed on and involve less bargaining costs. Again linking this argument to the context of European decision making the diversity of preferences could flow from the fact of an increasing number of member governments with diverse preferences deciding under unanimity rule. But it could also be related to the fact that by establishing the Parliament as a full co-legislator under co-decision, legislative decision making in the European Union became more costly in terms of negotiation costs. However, one might argue that just the opposite causal mechanism comes into play. Polities with few veto-players need *not* take recourse to delegation because their detailed decisions are less at risk of being blocked by veto-players. Whether one or the other causal mechanism comes into play would have to be subject to empirical scrutiny.

The shifting of responsibility or 'blame shifting' (Fiorina 1982) is another important reason for delegation that is discussed in the literature. If the electoral costs of regulation are expected to be greater than the benefits, a rational legislator would delegate rather than legislate. Like substantive uncertainty and the need for expertise, this motive of delegation has been linked to the specific features of a policy issue. Epstein and O'Halloran (1999) and Pollack (2003) analysed the link between the political benefits of a measure and the legislators' wish to delegate: if the policy in question implies concentrated benefits and widely dispersed costs, legislators are expected to shift the blame of the policy to bureaucrats and delegate. Conversely, if a measure entails concentrated costs and widely distributed benefits, they would prefer legislation.[7]

In conclusion, various motives may explain why principals delegate decision making to an agent, in this case the implementing powers of the Commission: policy uncertainty and need for expertise, political uncertainty and the need for policy credibility, as well as blame shifting.

Once legislators have decided to delegate, however, they also want to make sure that agents do not engage in 'shirking' behaviour. Ex ante incentives built into the contract may be one way to prevent agency shirking. Moreover, the application of ex post procedural controls over the agent may be needed (McCubbins et al. 1987; Miller 2005: 214).

---

[7] Delegation will also be preferred in 'no-win' areas with low political benefits in the case of success, but high political costs in the case of failure, such as air safety regulation (Epstein and O'Halloran 1999).

2.1.2 *Controlling the agent: The rules governing delegation*

Principals may engage in ex ante controls of the agent by inserting incentives into the contract that seek to align the agent's preferences with those of the principal. Principals may also introduce ex post controls by introducing specific rules controlling the behaviour of the agent while he/she is performing his/her obligations under the contract. The question of the principal's control over the agent, too, has been extensively dealt with in the literature on congressional oversight over bureaucracy. McCubbins et al. (1989) define bureaucratic discretion and latitude as those actions that no political coalition can overturn. Epstein and O'Halloran describe bureaucratic drift as 'the ability of an agency to enact outcomes different from the policies preferred by those who originally delegated power' (Epstein and O'Halloran 1999: 25). Devices of control to prevent agency drift may be included in the authorizing legislation. Such rules ('stacking the deck') imposed upon the agent are manifold: a prescription to privilege particular constituents' interests; the assigning of the burden of proof to one specific party; the prescription of consultation rules, rules of transparency, and public disclosure, which make it difficult for the agent to secretly mobilize against the principals' political objectives (McCubbins et al. 1987; Epstein and O'Halloran 1999).

Franchino, too, describes a number of instruments of ex ante control, such as time limits on delegation, spending limits, reporting requirements, consultation requirements, public hearings, rule-making requirements, appeals procedures, exemptions for individuals or classes of individuals, requirements for explicit legislative approval, and the possibility that the legislature may overrule an agent's decisions (Franchino 2004). McCubbins and Schwartz (1984) highlight mechanisms of ex post contractual control that allow a principal to discover problems of agency drift. Legislators can either seek to control bureaucrats by gathering their own information, or force the agent to disclose information at oversight hearing ('police patrol' oversight), or they can turn to those interest groups affected by the agent's decisions. These groups with the necessary expertise in their issue areas would have an incentive to let their representatives know when they find an agent's performance unsatisfactory ('fire alarm' oversight).

The existence of several principals has important implications for the control of the agent. Moe (1984) emphasized the importance of the separation of power and competitive partisan politics for the latitude of agent/bureaucracy. The existence of multiple principals enables the agent to play principals off against each other. However, as described above, principals are not helpless. They may lay down procedural rules in the contract that the agent has to follow and, additionally, they may rely on post-contract devices to keep the agent in line.

The relevance of these general arguments to the control of principals/member governments over the agent/Commission when delegating implementing powers is obvious. Comitology constitutes a system of ex ante contractual procedural rules allowing member states to control the Commission in producing secondary legislation. In participating in these committees, member governments ensure that their expertise is incorporated into secondary legislation and that legislation is applied in a uniform way across member states. The comitology rules are 'deck-stacking rules' and serve as an instrument of control. As described in Chapters 1 and 3, the procedural rules governing comitology vary in that they allow the Commission more or less latitude in the exercise of implementing powers. Until the Lisbon Treaty the Commission had a great deal of latitude under some procedures (advisory committees, management committees), and less under others (regulatory committees). As Steunenberg et al. (1996) conclude

> the advisory committee procedure, which does not restrict the Commission in the slightest way—the management committee procedure restricts the Commission the least. Under this implementation procedure,[8] the Commission has the most power in setting public policies. The Council would rank the current implementation procedure differently, that is, it would prefer the veto variant of the regulatory committee procedure most. (Steunenberg et al. 1996: 341)

With the new distinction between the 'Delegated Acts' and implementing acts introduced by the Lisbon Treaty, the nature of the instruments of control over the Commission in relation to implementing acts has changed. The changing of these rules governing comitology is at the centre of our investigation. We therefore turn to the theoretical explanation of the causes, processes, and outcomes of these changes, while details of the substantive changes will be analysed in Chapter 3.

2.2 Changing comitology rules: A power-based bargaining explanation

When raising the question about the change of rules governing comitology and, in particular, the efforts of the Parliament to gain more of a role in the process of delegation, we base our argument on bargaining

---

[8] i.e. under the Comitology Decision of 1987.

theories of institutional change (Héritier 2007). We assume that actors
are boundedly rational and seek to maximize their institutional power
in order to increase their influence over policy outcomes. At the same
time, actors are aware of their limits to process information and expertise, hence may find it desirable to delegate decision-making functions.
Faced with a conflict between the increase in institutional power on the
one hand, and seeing policy decisions speedily adopted on the other,
they may opt for the latter at the cost of the former. In other words, we
assume that actors, ceteris paribus, prefer to have important competences as compared to limited competences in a decision-making
procedure.

We further assume that actors interact in a given institutional context.
Institutions are defined as sets of man-made rules of behaviour that
facilitate and restrict social interactions (North 1990). They guide interaction in the accomplishment of joint tasks, such as legislation and
delegation. The existing rules allow the involved actors to incorporate
expectations with regard to the actions of other involved actors into
their own decision making (Lake and Powell 1999). This is because
actors assume that other actors will more or less abide by the existing
rules in order to avoid sanctions. Institutional rules, therefore, constitute an important source of information in forming expectations as to
how other actors are likely to behave.

Given bounded rationality and the transaction costs of information
collection and negotiation, these institutional rules are assumed to
constitute incomplete contracts,[9] which—in the course of their application—will be subject to renegotiation. Moreover, given uncertainty and
the lack of information about the actions and intentions of political
actors, and the impossibility of anticipating all possible future contin-
gencies, contracting partners are wary of the long-term distributional
consequences of their actions (Lake 1999; Koremenos et al. 2001). For
procedural reasons they therefore prefer incomplete contracts which
may be adjusted to changing circumstances, and hesitate to commit

---

[9] We are not basing our argument on Incomplete Contract Theory as developed by Grossman and Hart (1986), which studies the impact of an institutional framework on contract
design. Grossman and Hart's incomplete contract theory assumes actors' complete information in that they know the structure of all the problems that may occur and view the
future in terms of probabilities of the occurrence of issues. It argues that complete contracts
on actors' future actions are impossible when no third party can 'verify' ex post the real value
of the elements central to the contract of interaction (Brousseau and Glachant 2008). By
contrast we depart from the assumption of bounded rationality and incomplete information
as regards future states of the world and sequence of events and hence the impossibility to ex
ante negotiate complete contracts. Moreover, contracts may be left ambiguous for strategic
reasons in order to be able to renegotiate the costs and benefits of the contract in view of a
changed environment.

themselves to very specific and detailed contracts which fully specify all responsibilities and obligations of the contracting parties and seek to anticipate every possible future contingency (Cooley and Spruyt 2007: 8). For strategic reasons, moreover, actors may prefer incomplete contracts because they offer the possibility of correcting distributional asymmetries that may ensue from the initial agreement (Koremenos et al. 2001; Cooley and Spruyt 2007: 9). In addition, incomplete institutional rules only formulate general goals and hence are also more readily accepted by actors than well-specified and detailed rules (Héritier 1997).

We specifically focus on the distributional implications of institutional rules and ask how—given the distributional implications—a change of rule may come about. How does the distributional effect of a rule impact upon the preferences of the actors concerned? Are those disadvantaged by a rule able to modify it in a further renegotiation? If yes, under which conditions? We apply theoretical considerations to answer the question of why the institutional rules governing the Commission's implementing powers have changed over time and of how they influenced the preferences of the Commission, the Council, and the European Parliament. The changes focused on have taken the form of intentional, designed changes of formal rules *and* a subsequent alteration of these formal rules in the course of their application, which gives rise to informal institutional rules.

2.2.1 *Designed institutional change*

Designed institutional change is the result of an intentional act between two or more actors. The contract, that is, the institutional rule, is based on a voluntary agreement, an exchange among actors that facilitates mutually beneficial outcomes. Under the assumption of bounded rationality and the transaction costs of collecting information, negotiating, and monitoring contract compliance, the potential costs of negotiating an institutional rule are taken into account when considering the option. Newly designed governance rules are most likely to emerge when potential benefits are high and the transactions costs of developing, negotiating, monitoring, and enforcing the rules are low (Heckathorn and Maser 1987; Taylor and Singleton 1993). We further assume *actors are competence-maximizers,* who—while seeking to increase the efficiency of an institutional rule—also try to ensure that a policy will be enacted through procedures that maximize their own degree of control over the process of policymaking. They will therefore press for the widespread use of procedures that favour their own interests and—if powerful—will prevail in shaping the institutional rule. Hence, a change of institutional design considers the distributive effects that a specific governance rule would have for individual actors, a reasoning captured by distributive power-based bargaining theory. While the overall outcome may be beneficial to all the actors concerned (otherwise they would not have engaged in the institutional design in the first place), individual gains, however, may be distributed unevenly across individual actors.[10] In other words, institutions are assumed to have diverse distributional consequences for the involved actors (Knight 1992; Héritier 2007). Since there are always multiple possibilities of cooperation when dealing with a collective action problem, the selection of one institutional rule to achieve this goal will always be contested, precisely because of its distributive implications for individual actors (Snidal 1996: 125). The fact that in the designing of an institutional rule some actors win and others lose is accounted for by the relative power of an actor in the bargaining position over institutional rules and existing environmental conditions, such as the existing decision-making rule (Krasner 1991; Sebenius 1992; Knight 1995; Héritier 2007).

Bargaining power derives from asymmetries in resource ownership or, put another way, the availability of a fall-back position in the case of a breakdown of negotiations. Resource ownership affects the willingness of rational, self-interested actors to accept the bargaining demands of other actors. The most important resources are those available if the negotiations prove to be lengthy and costly or even unsuccessful (Knight 1995: 108). If an actor disposes of a comfortable fall-back position in the case of bargaining failure, he/she is less risk averse and more 'patient'; i.e. he/she is not pressed for time (Elster 1989b: 111–12; Knight 1992, 1995: 109).[11]

In negotiations over the design of institutional rules, the outcome will reflect the asymmetric resources of the actors who have been engaged in the bargaining process. The consideration of distributional effects renders the decision-making process more difficult and lengthy because

---

[10] By individual actors, we do not mean individuals as actors, but rather collective and corporate actors, such as the European Commission, the European Council, member state governments, the European Parliament.

[11] The (ex ante defined) power of an actor is reflected in his or her capacity to influence the feasible alternatives available to the other actors involved (Knight 1992: 41–2). This in turn depends on the actors' credibility, risk aversion, and time preferences (Bacharach and Lawler 1981; Raiffa 1982; Knight 1992: 131–2). Put differently, the more credible are the restrictions stated by an actor, the lower his or her risk aversion, the less intense the time pressure on an actor, and the better the fall-back position in the case of bargaining failure, the more powerful will he/she be in negotiations and in shaping the bargaining outcome (Elster 1989; Maynard Smith 1982: 153; Knight 1992: 127).

each actor will anticipate his or her likely benefits or losses linked to a specific institutional rule[12] (Fearon 1998). The potential losers of a proposed rule will seek to prevent its adoption (Riker 1980: 444–5). Whether or not they succeed in doing so depends on the support they can muster in the negotiation process. Since pre-existing institutions lend strategic advantage to those who control them, any attempt to change them must overcome considerable resistance (Sened 1991: 398). A change would come about if, induced by a change in the preferences of the most powerful actor(s) and a change in the balance of power between the involved actors (Lake 2004: 4), an existing change-resisting coalition breaks apart (Tsebelis 1990). It could also result from a change in the actors' bargaining power due to change in their resources or fall-back positions (Knight 1992) caused, in turn, by an exogenous event.

One may argue against the distributional power-based bargaining approach of institutional design that negotiation outcomes are not a *one-to-one reflection* of the relative bargaining power of particularly involved actors, but rather that extant institutional rules may have a power-transforming aspect, enhancing or detracting from the advantages of the most powerful (Snidal 1996: 127); for instance, the rules of agenda setting and the procedural sequence of decision making have an impact upon the bargaining process and its outcomes. A widely defined agenda, even under unanimity rule, may facilitate a linkage across multiple issues, and may thereby offer more possibilities of give-and-take through issue linkages and package deals for actor groups with diverse interests. It may even enable redistributive outcomes, an outcome that would be impossible under a single-issue agenda (Davis 2004: 153–4). Similarly, the definition of the decision sequence, and whether the decision-making rules provide for a separate decision on each issue or a single decision on *all* issues, is likely to make a significant difference as to how power translates into outcomes. In other words, the broadening of the scope of actors and interests can provide the impetus for change and the attenuation of power (Davis 2004: 154, 167). Or in general terms, actors dissatisfied with the status quo must *broaden* the scope of the institutional issues discussed, using the linkage of give-and-take to convince the (expected) losers to support a particular rule by compensating them in another issue area (Mitchell and Keilbach 2001: 892).

---

[12] De facto, however, most issues mix efficiency (wealth increasing) issues with distributive issues (Snidal 1996: 125).

Another important institutional condition for understanding the dynamics of a bargaining process is the question of whether we are dealing with one arena or linked arenas. In the case of linked arenas, the rationale of acting in one arena and its outcome is linked to the rationale of the other arena and its outcome. By making the outcome in one arena dependent on the outcome in another, actors take hostage of the decision-making process in the first arena. These institutional conditions in developing a power-based bargaining explanation of a change of rules governing delegation will be incorporated into our further argument.

While changing institutional rules by design and formal bargaining constitutes an important source of institutional change which also plays a role in the analysis of the transformation of rules governing comitology, there is also an avenue of more hidden institutional change that occurs informally and 'interstitially' between the formal redesigning events.

2.2.2 The emergence of informal institutions and interstitial institutional change

Starting out from the same assumptions of bounded rationality, transaction costs, and formal institutional rules as incomplete contracts (Farrell and Héritier 2003, 2004, 2006; Stacey and Rittberger 2003), and assuming that actors seek to maximize their institutional power, we further argue on the basis of power-based distributive negotiation theory that—contracts being incomplete—a *formal/informal dynamics* of institutional change may give rise to new informal institutional rules. The incompleteness of contracts/institutional rules flows from the high transaction costs of collecting information on possible circumstances of contract application, but also from the diversity of interests of the actors who are negotiating the initial formal institutional rule and strategic considerations. In order to save transaction costs of negotiating, and—given diversity of preferences—to allow for agreement at all, actors often settle for rather vague rule formulations. Morover, as discussed above, actors may prefer incomplete contracts because they offer the possibility of correcting distributional asymmetries that may ensue from the initial agreement (Koremenos et al. 2001; Cooley and Spruyt 2007: 9).

As a result—due to the ambiguity of the institutional formal rule and possible external events—in the course of its application the formal rule will be subject to renegotiation and may give rise to an informal institutional rule. An informal institutional rule is defined as a non-written institutional rule that has been generated outside the official channels of rule creation (Helmke and Levitsky 2004: 725, 727), that is not subject to third party dispute resolution and *formal* sanctions in the case of non-compliance (Farrell and Héritier 2003, 2004).[13]

Informal rules emerging in the course of rule application may be of a distributive nature, i.e. they may affect the decision-making power of the involved actors, *or* they may be of a mere efficiency-increasing nature, i.e. all are better off due to their application, with benefits evenly distributed.

INFORMAL INSTITUTIONS: SHIFTING POWER

We submit that the redefinition of the initial formal rule takes the form of an implicit bargaining process and reflects the relative power of the actors involved. Certain institutional factors determine the relative power of the actors: First, there are the actors' formal institutional positions in the decision-making process at t1, which define each actor's competence and thereby influence his/her ability to credibly threaten specific kinds of action. One example would be the unanimity rule which gives the right of veto to every actor. Further institutional conditions, such as the fact of whether decision making occurs across multiple arenas, or whether it is a multiple issue agenda or not, and in which sequence voting occurs, may also determine the outcome of the bargaining process. Ultimately, given the institutional conditions, an actor's available fall-back position if negotiations should fail will determine the negotiated informal rule. The longer an actor's time horizon, and the lower the intensity of his/her preferences, the more powerful he/she will be in the bargaining process. Such power enables him/her to make credible threats with regard to this item (or items) of negotiation in order to enhance his/her overall position in the bargaining process (Elster 1989b; Knight 1995). In short, the informal rules that provide a modified basic structure of interaction and changing the status quo of institutional guidance will reflect the differential power of actors to make credible threats.

INFORMAL INSTITUTIONS: INCREASING EFFICIENCY

Alternatively, given ambiguous formal institutions, the emergence of informal institutions may be accounted for by the efficiency-increasing nature of informal rules. Actors agree on an informal rule by voluntarily

---

[13] By contrast, formal institutional rules are usually written down ('parchment' [Carey 2000]), created in the formal channels of political decision making and are subject to third party dispute resolution. They are monitored and—in case of non-abidance—formal sanctions may ensue.

coordinating themselves. Since actors prefer coordination to non-coordination they are willing to use salient information to achieve this coordination by means of an institutional rule coordinating around this salient information (Ullman-Margalit 1978; Sugden 1986). The informal rule saves transaction costs and is of a complementary or accommodating nature (Helmke and Levitsky 2004: 728) with respect to the formal rule. Since it is beneficial to all the actors concerned, it is self-enforcing. No unequal distribution of costs and benefits is linked to such an informal institutional rule.

2.2.3 *Formalizing informal institutional rules*

Once an informal institutional rule has developed, the question is whether it will be sustained and even formalized. The informal rule which brings about a power shift depends on the continuing support of a coalition of powerful actors. In the case of the efficiency-enhancing informal rules beneficial to all actors, it will be sustained as long as it is considered to be beneficial. We may expect a formalization of an informal institutional rule when all actors agree that the rule is beneficial to all (Farrell and Héritier 2004). In the case of a power-shifting informal rule the empowered actors may obtain a formalization—even under unanimity—if the latter establish an issue linkage and threaten to block a decision in another political arena (Héritier 2007). More specifically, we assume at least two decision-making arenas, an arena X in which institutional rules are decided upon, and an arena Y in which substantive policies are decided upon; we further distinguish between actors (A) with decision competences relating to both arenas X and Y, i.e. institutional rules and substantive policies, and actors (B) with competences only relating to arena Y, i.e. substantive policies. We contend that (i) actors will seek to increase their institutional competences to influence policy outcomes by applying a formal veto in a decision-making arena of institutional design; (ii) actors B who have no formal veto in the arena of institutional design X will use their formal veto power in the substantive policy arena Y in which actors A also have a say. By linking the two arenas X and Y, and by withholding support for an issue in the substantive policy arena Y, actors B exert pressure and indirectly influence outcomes in the arena of institutional design X (in which they do not have a formal say). Applied to the Parliament, we argue that when the Parliament puts pressure on both the Commission and the Council, and threatens to withhold its support for a substantive legislative matter in the co-decision and/or budgetary arenas, it can indirectly influence the shaping of comitology rules in the arena of institutional design.

2.3 Power-based bargaining theory and principal–agent approach

As described above, our theoretical argument to account for the change of institutional rules governing comitology and the shift of power linked to these changes as regards the role of the Parliament builds on distributive power-based bargaining theory, and *not* principal–agent theory which has been predominantly used to explain the 'why' and 'how' of delegation to comitology.

While both theoretical approaches are based on rationalism, they are also based on slightly different behavioural assumptions: principal–agent theory is based on the utility efficiency maximizing actor, whereas we base our argument on the assumption of actors seeking to maximize their institutional power (in order to influence policy outcomes). Based on these divergent assumptions one would come to different predictions with regard to outcomes. For instance, assuming the efficiency orientation of actors we would predict that the Council, after the Commission's empowerment under the Comitology Decision of 1999, in order 'to get things done', would continue to favour delegation over legislation. Based on the power-maximizing assumption—by contrast—we hypothesize that the Council will hesitate to delegate under conditions of increased Commission power. Whether one of the other claims holds is a question of empirical testing. Or to give another example: with co-decision and an additional principal (the Parliament), principal–agent theory would predict an increased use of delegation, while distributive bargaining theory predicts the opposite. Our results will show that the truth is in between: the Parliament does not oppose delegation, but systematically restricts its scope. In other words, both competence maximizing and efficiency-oriented behaviour produce different predictions. Both reflect crucial actor orientations between which there may be a trade-off; actors insisting on maximizing their institutional power may come to unsatisfactory policy solutions; and actors with only the best policy solution in mind may lose in institutional power. In the conclusion of the book, implications of the different approaches will be discussed in the light of empirical findings.

2.4 An alternative explanation: Sociological institutionalism

Other accounts of why informal rules emerge from formal rules emphasize causal mechanisms entirely different from the ones invoked by rational choice bargaining theory and rational functional consider-ations. From a sociological institutionalist perspective (March and Olsen 1989; Sverdrup 2005), informal institutional rules result from a process of arguing and deliberation over unclear formal institutional rules. The emerging informal rules are subsequently passed on through socialization processes to other actors (Joerges and Neyer 1997a; Puett-ner 2003). In informal communication, political actors routinize and 'communize' the process of interpretation of institutional rules (Joerges and Neyer 1997a; Puettner 2003: 115). Following Habermas (1987), it is maintained that arguing and deliberation is about truth-seeking which occurs if actors retreat from a strategic position after being persuaded by a discourse that invokes a particular set of shared values of rationality and impartiality (Puettner 2003: 116). Like Checkel (2001c) and Risse (2000), Puettner contends that arguing which drives the emergence of informal institutional rules is more likely to occur in a closed setting under conditions of confidentiality and without being subject to public scrutiny (Puettner 2003: 117); Joerges and Neyer (1997a), Wessels (1998), and Dehousse (2003), explicitly focusing on institutional rules applied in comitology, develop such a sociologically institutionalist argument and describe comitology as a forum in which experts meet and discuss in order to develop the best solution to the policy problem at hand. What prevails in comitology is deliberation or 'problem solving' based on persuasion. Actors are persuaded by the 'better' argument providing substantive evidence for a debate backed by scientific evidence, rather than engaging in a power-driven bargaining process within given formal voting and organizational rules. Joerges and Neyer 1997 call this process 'deliberative supranationalism' in which formal structures are expected to be of limited importance (1997: 288). Comitology, moreover, has a socializing effect on its members, since actors by working together over extended periods of time develop a common understanding of problems and solutions and 'move from representa-tives of the national interest to representatives of a Europeanized administrative discourse in which mutual learning and understanding for each others' difficulties surrounding the implementation of standards become of central importance' (Joerges and Neyer 1997: 291; see also Lewis 2003, 2005). In an empirical survey of 294 Dutch and Danish members of comitology committees, Brandsma and Blom-Hansen (2011) find that depending on the issues at stake committees tend to use more deliberation or bargaining.

> Handling cases with distributive effects or cases that are technically complex drives the committees towards a bargaining interaction style. If business takes a strong interest in the committees' work this also leads to a bargaining climate. In contrast, bargaining is reduced if the representatives have participated in their committee for a long time … Deliberation … is positively associated with the handling of technically complex cases … but we fail to find any impact of socialization. (Blom-Hansen and Brandsma 2009: 736)

Similarly Bradley (1997), Toeller (1998), and Gehring (1999) find that the daily work of comitology committees and the institutional rules governing these daily workings are characterized both by intergovernmental bargaining and deliberation and the exchange of good arguments (Blom-Hansen 2011a, b: 612). Along a similar line of reasoning Christiansen and Kirchner (2000) argue that committees are

> an expression of, and a catalyst for, decision-making based on consensus and consultation in EU decision-making … Given … the substantial amounts of time which is spent by national officials in EU committees—this feeds into a … process of cultural learning: … committees provide the central institutions with an ability to observe at first hand, … the cultural diversity in European public administration (Christiansen and Kirchner 2000: 9) … ideally governed by deliberative rationality. (Weale 2000: 169)

With respect to our research question of why the Parliament was increasingly empowered in delegated legislation, a sociologically institutionalist argument would claim that democratic norms urging the inclusion of the Parliament in these decision-making processes became ever more pressing and eventually led to a change of institutional rules. While accepting that socialization and deliberation processes and the power of democratic values are a possible source of institutional change favouring the increasing role of Parliament in comitology, the question remains why it took so long before these democratic norms made an impact. And why did the Parliament time and time again actively threaten to block the legislative process and budgetary process in order to underline its requests for more institutional power? A power-based institutionalist argument—in our view—holds more explanatory power when it comes to account for this amazing institutional career of the Parliament. In methodological terms we choose to empirically assess the explanatory power of *one* theory, i.e. rational choice institutionalism, with respect to our explanandum, instead of trying to account for 100 per cent of the variation of the dependent variable by sequentially including several diverse theories. As will be shown empirically, the chosen theoretical approach offers considerable explanatory traction.

2.5 Hypotheses

From the theoretical argument on distributive power-based bargaining discussed above, we draw a number of hypotheses which will guide our empirical research on actors' preferences for specific institutional rules and the changing of the rules governing comitology. We generally assume that actors are competence maximizers—that is, they will seek to ensure that policy will be enacted through procedures which maximize their own degree of control over the process of policymaking, and not through procedures where they have little or no control. In other words, we argue that actors' preferences over delegation will be determined by the degree to which they have effective influence over policy that is carried out through delegation as opposed to legislation. As a result, they will press for the widespread use of procedures that favour their own interests and for less frequent use (and, where possible, the alteration or abandonment) of those procedures that do not.

More specifically, we argue that actors' preferences regarding delegation, *under given institutional rules*, will be a function of whether the actor has more ability to influence policy through delegation or through legislation, and that those preferences change as the attractiveness of pursuing legislation or delegation changes (Bergström et al. 2007). In the EU, given the distribution of competences described in Chapter 1, we expect that the relevant collective actors will have the following preferences regarding delegation.

The *Commission* will, in general, prefer extensive delegation, with minimal or no control by member states; in other words, it would prefer the advisory committee procedure which is not linked with restrictions, and the management committee which restricts the Commission the least (Steunenberg et al. 1996: 341). However, its preferences will to some extent depend on the availability of alternative forms of policy-making through legislation. In periods when the Commission has difficulty proposing legislation that has good prospects of being adopted, it may be more amenable to extensive member state control in delegation than it would otherwise be.

The *European Parliament* will prefer legislation (especially under co-decision) over delegation since—until very recently—its competences in comitology were almost non-existent, while under legislation it can exert influence on the content of the decision.[14] If delegation was chosen, the

---

[14] Even under the consultation procedure, the Parliament has the power to delay its opinion for a certain amount of time and may thereby take influence on the content of the legislative draft.

Parliament traditionally supported the Commission in its endeavours to work under the least restrictive comitology procedures, i.e. the advisory committee or the management committee procedures. It also has traditionally been opposed to the use of the regulatory committee procedures.

Finally, the *Council* will generally prefer the consultation procedure, or delegation, as opposed to legislation under co-decision, because this allows it to maximize its institutional power (see also Steunenberg et al. 1996: 341). As we have seen in the summary of the principal–agent literature on the 'why' of delegation, member states in the Council may have many reasons to delegate: substantive uncertainty and the need for expertise; political uncertainty in both the sense of trying to reduce the risk of not arriving at an agreement in the light of highly diverse preferences; but also to ensure political credibility in the sense of tying down their successor governments to specific policies; and finally, the motivation to shift the blame for politically unpopular decisions.

Given these assumptions, we argue that the actors' preferences for delegation will be dependent on a given institutional rule, and hence would shift when the rule changes. More specifically, we expect that the preferences of actors regarding whether or not to delegate will depend on their competences under delegation. Accordingly, actors will modify their preferences for delegation when the procedures governing delegation or legislation are changed in a way that shifts the competences between actors. The actor(s) who gained competences under delegation will increasingly opt for delegation, whereas the actor(s) who suffered a relative loss in competences will not choose delegation.

Changing the institutional rules governing comitology

How did the institutional rules develop that increasingly empowered the Parliament? As described in the general theory, we assume that actors are boundedly rational competence maximizers, and that transaction costs and diversity of member state preferences lead to incomplete contracts. From these assumptions we conclude that a given formal institutional rule defining the formal distribution of competences in legislation and delegation will be ambiguous and subject to subsequent renegotations. The losing actors will try to shift the decision-making weight in their favour between formal treaty revisions. They may achieve this interstitial shift of power by changing the division between legislation and delegation or by changing the rules governing delegation.

To understand the processes through which preferences are translated into outcomes, we invoke a common mechanism—bargaining—in a *given institutional context*. Since the bargaining power of actors changes with altered formal institutional rules at the treaty level, these formal rules influence their preferences for delegation or legislation, depending on whether they can exert more influence on policymaking through delegation rather than legislation. The extant institutional rules also determine their ability to prevail in conflicts over delegation and in their renegotation between formal rule changes. Actors' bargaining strength will ultimately depend on the credible threats to impede or veto legislative measures, threats that they may make to back up their arguments. In order to make such a threat, the actor in question has to (a) have the de facto ability to impede, or (better yet) to block, specific items of legislation, and (b) be less sensitive to the impeding or blocking of the legislation in question than are the other relevant actors.

To summarize, when asking why and how the Parliament set out to hold back delegation, and under which conditions it successfully attained more institutional competences in comitology, we assume the existence of several linked[15] decision-making arenas either of institutional design or substantive policymaking. We contend that: (i) utility maximizing actors will seek to increase institutional competences to influence policy outcomes by applying a formal veto in a decision-making arena of institutional design; (ii) if they have no formal veto in the arena of institutional design, actors will use the formal veto power in another central substantive decision-making arena in order to exert pressure and indirectly influence outcomes in the arena of institutional design. Applied to the Parliament, we argue that when the Parliament puts pressure on both the Commission and the Council, and threatens to withhold its support for a substantive legislative matter in the co-decision and/or budgetary arenas, it can exert indirect influence on the shaping of comitology rules in the arena of institutional design. In order to widen the possibilities of favourable outcomes it also can turn to the ECJ (European Court of Justice – the Court) and hope for a ruling in its favour. However, the outcome of a new Court ruling cannot be strategically anticipated because preferences of the Court cannot be defined ex ante.

This leads us to the following propositions:

H1 If the Parliament uses bargaining leverage across linked arenas and makes its support for substantive co-decision issues dependent on the other actors' acceptance to legislate instead of delegate, it will obtain more legislation.

[15] 'linked' in the sense that actors in one arena are dependent on decisions taken by actors in the other arena and that some actors are formally deciding in both arenas: e.g. member governments decide in a co-decision process on the one hand and member governments decide in a Council decision the rules governing comitology on the other.

H2 If the Parliament uses bargaining leverage across linked arenas, i.e. links its support for substantive co-decision issues with demands for institutional reform of comitology procedures, it will obtain an increase in competences under comitology.

After the longitudinal qualitative analysis of institutional change of the rules governing comitology from the angle of the Parliament's influence, we turn to a quantitative test of our arguments about institutional changes and institutional preferences. We focus on two important changes of institutional rules. The first was the introduction of co-decision establishing the Parliament as a second legislator. We expect that the introduction of co-decision rendered delegation— where the Parliament was absent until very recently—more attractive to the Commission and to the Council. The second significant change was the reform of the Comitology Decision in 1999 which increased the competences of the Commission in comitology procedures. We expect that the Council—given a relative loss of control over the Commission—would tend to delegate less. As regards the Parliament we expect that with co-decision it will be disinclined to support delegation.

In more detail, with the introduction of co-decision, the Commission has to take into account a second legislator that may or may not support its proposal. By comparison, under delegation, the Commission—until recently—did not have to reckon with the possibility of a rejection of its decision by the Parliament. In addition, the Commission is much stronger under comitology procedures than under co-decision. This particularly holds for the advisory and management committees, but also—to some extent—for the regulatory committees. In regulatory committees, the Commission was able to set time limits by which the committee had to deliver its opinion. If the Council failed to adopt or annul the proposal by QMV, the proposal was adopted within three months. Co-decision, by contrast, is the legislative procedure under which the Commission's powers suffered a relative loss. This is because, in the conciliation committee, the Council may amend the Commission's proposal with a qualified majority rather than the usual unanimity. Co-decision is also the longest procedure, which could turn out to be problematic for proposals that the Commission would like to see adopted quickly. For the above reasons, we assume that the Commission has a preference for delegation over co-decision,[16] and we submit that:

H3 With increasing legislative competences of the Parliament under co-decision, the Commission will be more inclined to propose delegation to comitology.

---

[16] Napel and Widgrén (2008) ascertained that Commission policies are, on average, more in accord with the aggregate position of the Parliament than with that of the Council.

With regard to the type of comitology procedure, the Commission is of two minds. On the one hand it has a preference for a comitology procedure that involves the least control by the Council, i.e. the advisory or management procedures. On the other hand it also anticipates the Council's opposition to these types of procedure for Delegated Acts that could alternatively be adopted solely through legislation.[17] In other words, the Commission—aware of the divergent preferences of the Council and the fact that the Council can overturn the Commission's choice of committee—does not seek to realize its meta-preferences, but strategically pursues its second-best option, i.e. its situational preferences (Frieden 1999).

We therefore submit two further hypotheses:

H4 With an increasing number of delegation proposals, the Commission will propose the least constraining procedures, i.e. advisory and management committees

H IV With an increasing number of delegation proposals, the Commission will propose the more restrictive comitology procedure, i.e. regulatory committees.

With regard to the Council, with the introduction of the co-decision procedure, member states in the Council suffered a relative loss of influence in the legislative procedure. By contrast, their influence in the control of the Commission's implementing powers has remained untouched.[18] Under co-decision, it will therefore prefer delegation to the Commission along with extensive control by the member states. Based on the assumption that actors seek to increase their institutional power, we therefore expect that, with the introduction of co-decision, in order to protect its own institutional power, the Council will be more inclined to delegate legislative powers to the Commission. In other words, actors who have to share decision-making power with a new actor seek to avoid sharing this power, and delegation offers such a possibility.

H5 With increasing legislative competences of the Parliament under co-decision, the Council will be inclined to delegate more to comitology.

---

[17] The likely objection of the Council to the advisory and management committees may be derived from the Council's Comitology Decision, which states that regulatory committees should be used in the case of 'measures of general scope designed to apply essential provisions of basic instruments' and to the updating or adaptation of 'certain non-essential provisions of the instrument'.

[18] One could ask why the Council delegated the power to issue implementing decisions to the Commission in the first place. As will be shown in the longitudinal analysis (Chapter 3), member states were faced with a trade-off between efficiency on the one hand and yielding decision-making power to the Commission on the other. To decide all detailed issues of secondary legislation itself would have quickly exhausted the Council's capacity.

Different types of comitology procedures imply different distributions of competences between member states and the Commission (and, most recently, the Parliament). The voting rule for only one of these procedures—the regulatory procedure—requires a qualified majority, as is the case for legislation presented in the Council. In the two other committees—the advisory and the management committees—member states only give their advice or—alternatively—need to obtain a qualified majority to *reject* the proposal. Hence, according to our above assumption, we would expect that, if the Council wishes to delegate more in order to circumvent the Parliament, it would want to link the increase in delegation to the use of the regulatory procedure.

> *H6 The increase in delegation accepted by the Council will be accompanied by an increase in the use of the regulatory committee.*

Based on our assumption that the Parliament will prefer legislation (especially under co-decision) over delegation, we expect that—with the introduction of co-decision—the EP will be even keener to insist on legislation and oppose delegation.

> *H7 With increasing legislative competences of the Parliament under co-decision, the Council will be inclined to delegate more to comitology.*

In a further quantitative analytical step we scrutinize the effect of another institutional rule change on actors' preferences for the extent and mode of delegation under comitology, i.e. the Second Comitology Decision of 1999. This institutional change brought a relative empowerment of the Commission vis-à-vis the Council. We therefore expect corresponding changes of preferences by the Commission and the Council. The Second Comitology Decision abolished two committee procedures that implied particularly restrictive national controls vis-à-vis the Commission. It is therefore plausible to expect that after the repeal of these procedures the Commission would more frequently propose delegating legislation.

With regard to the specific type of comitology procedure, we expect that—after the adoption of the Second Comitology Decision—the Commission would be more willing than before to submit to the oversight of management and regulatory committees because the restrictive variants of the corresponding procedures will have been abolished. However, as argued above—the Commission—in view of the opposed Council preferences and the ultimate right of the Council to select a committee—does not seek to realize its meta-preferences, but strategically pursues its second-best option and would propose delegating legislation in a regulatory committee.

Finally, with the Comitology Decision of 1999, member states in the Council suffered a relative loss of influence in comitology, whereas their influence on legislation remained untouched. Given our assumption that actors seek to maximize their institutional power to increase their influence over policy outcomes, we may therefore expect that, with the adoption of the Second Comitology Decision, the Council would, in order to protect its own institutional power, be less inclined to delegate legislative powers to the Commission.

We therefore submit that:

H8 After the adoption of the Second Comitology Decision, the Commission will more frequently propose delegation of implementing powers under the regulatory and management procedures.

H9 After the adoption of the Second Comitology Decision, the increase in Commission proposals delegating proposals to regulatory committees will be higher than those delegated to management committees.

H10 After the adoption of the Second Comitology Decision, the Council will more frequently reject Commission delegation proposals to management and regulatory committees.

In concluding this theoretical chapter, we depart from the principal–agent literature that focuses on why principals delegate and how they seek to control the agent, and analyse delegation from the angle of power distribution among the involved actors, the Council, the Commission, and the Parliament. We base our argument on institutionalist power-based bargaining theory and argue that all actors seek to establish a mode of decision making that maximizes their institutional power; and ask whether, if dissatisfied with a formal delivery of competence distribution, they will seek to alter through a re-bargaining of these during the application of the rules. We particularly focus on the rising power of the Parliament, and the way in which it changes the parameters of the contest for power, in order to explain why the role of the Parliament in the governance of comitology has changed over time.

3

Changing the rules of comitology: More competences for the Parliament

3.1 Hypotheses

Initially the Parliament played no role in the comitology system. Today the Parliament has a co-equal right to object to Commission delegating acts (Art. 290 TFEU) and to shape the comitology decision with the Council (Art. 291). How did this change in the institutional rules governing comitology come about? Redistributive bargaining theory may explain these changes. If the Parliament uses bargaining leverage across linked arenas and makes its support for substantive co-decision questions and budget questions depend on a change of comitology rules, it will obtain an increase in competences under comitology.

As developed in the theoretical chapter, we assume multiple decision-making arenas and we distinguish between actors (A) with decision competences relating to both institutional rules and substantive policies; and actors (B) with only substantive policy competences. We contend that (i) utility maximizing actors will seek to increase their institutional competences to influence policy outcomes by applying a formal veto in a decision-making arena of institutional design. (ii) Actors B who have no formal veto in the arena of institutional design will use their formal veto power in the substantive policy arena in which actors A also have a say. By linking the two arenas, and by withholding support for an issue in the substantive policy arena, actors B exert pressure and indirectly influence outcomes in the arena of institutional design (in which they do not have a formal say). Applied to the Parliament, we argue that when the Parliament puts pressure on both the Commission and the Council, and threatens to withhold its support for a substantive legislative matter in the co-decision and/or budgetary arenas, it can indirectly influence the shaping of comitology rules in the arena of institutional design.

We therefore propose that:

H1 If the Parliament uses bargaining leverage across linked arenas and makes its support for substantive co-decision questions depend on whether other actors agree to legislate instead of delegate, it will secure more legislation.

H2 If the Parliament uses bargaining leverage across linked arenas, i.e. if it links its support for substantive co-decision questions with demands for institutional reform of comitology procedures, it will secure an increase in competences under comitology.

By empirically investigating the role of the Parliament in the development of comitology rules over time we will make a plausibility probe of this argument. We will distinguish different periods under which comitology rules have undergone a clear change—each period ending by a rule change, and, applying a backward-looking design, we empirically scrutinize how those reforms affected the Parliament, and then proceed to identify the relevant factors accounting for the outcome in the light of our two hypotheses. If arena linking by the Parliament plays an important role in accounting for the outcome of a given period, we will consider this to be a tentative confirmation of our conjectures.

Considering the development of the institutional rules governing the role of the Parliament in comitology over the last forty years, how can we account for their transformation?[1] How did these transformations affect the role of the Parliament, and how did the Parliament try to play a role in the shaping of these rules?

3.2 The European Parliament in comitology: From the beginnings until the Lisbon Treaty

In the shaping of the original comitology system between 1957 and 1961, the Parliament did not have a role to play. After a period of institutional contest, in 1961 the Council and the Commission settled on a *management committee* system (Council Regulation 1962), providing that common organizations were to be established for the markets in cereals, pork, eggs, poultry, fruit and vegetables, and wine. Since the Parliament saw its power of political supervision of the Commission indirectly affected, it requested—but to no avail—that its opinion be

---

[1] For an analysis of the institutional tensions in the development of the comitology system see also Alfé and Christiansen (2009: 49–69) and Christiansen and Vaccari (2009: 333–51).

heard and that the Commission should assume sole political responsibility for the new organs of cooperation (Deringer Report [1962: 33–5]). Yet the Parliament, having no veto player lever to bring its influence to bear across arenas (*H1*), did not have any impact on the decision outcomes.

From CAP, comitology was extended to commercial policy, for which the Commission proposed also to use the management committee. But governments insisted on a new, more restrictive formula, the *regulatory committees*, allowing the adoption of a decision only after prior approval by member states by qualified majority. If it failed to act, the Commission could proceed with its decision (*filet* or safety net). In an additional area, foodstuffs, again the Commission proposed to operate under management committees, but some member states insisted on even stricter control under a new 'double safety net' or *contre-filet* procedure allowing the Council (by a simple majority) to prevent the Commission from acting, even if the Council had not decided within a certain period (Joerges and Neyer 1997).

The Parliament criticized this type of committee, deplored a surge in legislative matters dealt with as implementing measures, and proposed systematic criteria to be followed in allocating measures to advisory, management, and regulatory committees.[2] Moreover, it requested a *droit de regard* to be informed about decision drafts and the right to state an opinion whenever it considered that a draft was not merely a matter of technical implementation. Again, since the Parliament had no blocking power of decisions in one arena (*H1*), its requests were all but ignored by the Commission and the Council. In this situation it resorted to the ECJ and brought legal action against a Commission decision (Case 41/69, *Chemiefarma v Commission*), arguing that this decision was of a legislative nature. However, the Court in this case, and in another ruling (Case 25/70, *Einfuhr – und Vorratsstelle für Getreide – und Futtermittel v Köster, Berodt & Co*), adopted a wide interpretation of what constitutes an implementing measure. Hence, the Parliament's attempt to include another actor who might have thrown its weight behind its request to change the institutional rules governing comitology failed.

To summarize, in these first two periods in which the different comitology procedures were established, the Parliament only played a marginal role. It regarded the new procedures as a threat to its own status and to its right to exercise political control over the Commission. In the implicit negotiation among the three actors, the Commission did not side with the Parliament against the Council because it had much to

---

[2] Jozeau-Marigné Report, EP Doc n. 115/1968–69, 30 September 1968.

gain through the introduction of the committee system. Although it had to share the new competencies under comitology with national governments, the new mechanisms nevertheless conferred on it considerable institutional power. With no formal say in the adoption of the comitology decision, no ally, and no indirect veto power through a linked arena (such as legislation or budgetary authority) from which to gain bargaining clout, the Parliament had little impact on the shaping of the comitology rules. As shown above, it did seek the support of the Court to settle the institutional conflict over the rules governing comitology and the scope of delegation. The outcome, however, only boosted the institutional position of member states.

When, in the 1970s, attempts to create an economic and monetary union were caught up in a legislative deadlock (Nicoll 1998), the Council widened the mandate of COREPER (*Comité des représentants permanents*) and conferred additional implementing powers on the Commission. The comitology machinery continued to churn out implementing decisions. In particular, the regulatory committees grew rapidly in number (from six in 1970 to forty-six in 1980) and the Parliament—more than ever—saw its own institutional position undermined; on the other hand, it also saw that without regulatory committees there would be no integration progress at all. Therefore, rather than blocking the further use of regulatory committees, it sought to create a role for itself in the decision-making process.[3]

With the prospect of Southern enlargement (1981 and 1986), institutional reform came on the agenda. The Parliament proposed a 'Draft Treaty establishing the European Union' (DTEU) to be adopted in an Intergovernmental Conference. It was particularly concerned by the recent increase of comitology committees from 85 (1980) to 154 (1985) and proposed that new 'laws' should be introduced—comitology committees would be of an advisory nature only—and called for a *droit de regard* and a right of opinion. To underline its requests it made a first, if weak, attempt, to use cross-arena linkage (*H2*): it used its consultation right to delay legislation and its powers of budgetary control, freezing the committee funds (EP Resolution of 16.9.1983).[4] As a result the Commission provided the requested information, but refused to grant the Parliament a *droit de regard* (Bradley 1997: 232).

The daunting workload, linked to the completion of the internal market (297 proposals for the removal of non-tariff barriers), more

---

[3] See Jozeau-Marigné Report.

[4] In 1975 the Parliament's budgetary control in non-obligatory expenditure had been increased and a concertation procedure introduced.

than ever pointed to the need for institutional reform. In the *Single European Act* (SEA) member states acquiesced to a non-binding declaration that the advisory committee should be given priority to speed up the establishment of the internal market. The SEA also requested the adoption of a comitology decision. A Commission decision draft of 1987 proposed advisory, management, and regulatory committees linked to particular matters. The Parliament, in its Haensch Report, criticized the management and the regulatory committees for endangering 'the institutional balance' and circumventing the Parliament. It proposed to abolish the regulatory committee. In order to emphasize its demand, it delayed the decision by not delivering a formal opinion until the Commission brought its draft more into line with the Parliament's position, whereupon the Parliament delivered its opinion.

The Council, by contrast, in its Decision (87/373/EEC) of 1987, accepted almost nothing of the proposal. It even added the *contre-filet* procedure, which allowed for more member state control. In response, the Parliament stepped up its battle, stating:

> In first reading, Parliament should systematically delete any provisions for procedure III(a) or (b) (*filet et contre-filet*) and for proposals concerning the internal market put forward under Art. 100a of the EEC Treaty... In second reading Parliament should... oppose any provisions in a common position for procedure III(b). (Guidelines quoted in Corbett 1998: 258)

Yet under consultation and cooperation procedures the Parliament had little leverage in the Council's decision, i.e. the conditions described in *H1* and *H2*, as arena linkages were not given.

The Treaty of the European Union of 1991 and co-decision brought a sea change. It gave the Parliament a veto power in legislation which it hastened to use. In preparing the Intergovernmental Conference (IGC) that would lead to the Treaty on the European Union, the Commission proposed a hierarchy of legal acts (Bulletin ECD Supplement 2-1991): for 'laws' adopted by the Council, the Parliament would lay down general guidelines and provide the basis for decisions or regulations by the Commission. The regulatory committee would be abolished and replaced by a substitution mechanism, allowing the Council and the Parliament to legislate if the Commission should exceed its powers.

During the first year of co-decision, the Parliament fought over each individual item of legislation (Corbett 1998: 258, 347, 348) replacing the regulatory committee by an advisory committee. To overcome the stalemate the Council Presidency proposed a compromise, the *modus vivendi*. In bargaining the *modus vivendi*, Parliament—to underline its request—established a cross-arena link between the *modus vivendi* and the budget process and placed committee funds in the reserves. In response, governments acknowledged a de facto *droit de regard* of the Parliament in 1994. The Council, for the first time, committed itself directly to the Parliament in comitology matters.

In short, according to the expectations of *H2*, with co-decision the Parliament now had an instrument to force the other actors, in particular the Council, to pay more heed to its institutional demands. By engaging in arena linkage, making its acquiescence to a substantive co-decision matter contingent on the acceptance of its institutional demands regarding the rules governing comitology, it forced its negotiating partners to take seriously its proposals for rule revisions.

When preparing the Amsterdam Treaty member states committed themselves only to amend the first Comitology Decision. The Commission proposed general criteria for choosing different procedures; a substitution mechanism for regulatory procedures and a formalization of the *droit de regard*. The Parliament in its Aglietta Report called for a limitation of delegation, a formal voice in comitology decisions under co-decision and a repeal mechanism. When the Council refused to accept the demands, the Parliament warned

> the Council that...if the working group continues to be so restrictive on Parliament's rights to intervene, then there will be no agreement and we will continue in legislative procedure after legislative procedure to block the comitology measures and resist the adoption of such restrictive measures and we will be very restrictive on voting the budgets and the credits to allow comitology-type committees to continue to meet. (Corbett, Debates EP 5.5.1999)

The outcome was that the Council abolished the restrictive variant of the management committee and regulatory committee. Parliament was given the right to alert the Commission if it felt that a proposed decision was exceeding the implementing powers of the Commission, and the droit de regard became legally binding. In consequence, the Parliament released the appropriations that had been held in reserve. Again the Parliament held the member states and the Commission hostage in order to obtain a change of institutional rules, as expected under *H2*.

In the period that followed the *Treaty of Amsterdam (1997)* up to the *Second Comitology Decision of 1999*, the Commission, as required by the Amsterdam Treaty, submitted a proposal for a revision of the First Comitology Decision. Yet instead of proposing amendments, it submitted an entirely new set of rules for existing and future committees: under the regulatory committee procedure, if a draft implementing measure was not approved by the committee, the Commission would present a normal legislative proposal. This would abolish the controversial *contre-filet* mechanism, would strengthen the Commission's right of initiative, and allow for more parliamentary control. The Commission also proposed general criteria for choosing different procedures and the formalization of the Parliament's *droit de regard*.

When consulted the Parliament stated that too many matters were dealt with under delegation, thereby undermining the co-decision procedure. It also asked for a formal say in comitology decisions under co-decision and the insertion of a mechanism that would make it possible to repeal a measure. It also requested the abolition of the regulatory committee. While the Commission offered the Parliament a safeguard right to 'blow the whistle', the Council rejected all demands.

Eventually, the Council accepted a simplification of the comitology procedures, albeit not along the ambitious lines proposed by the Commission. Under the management committee procedure, the restrictive variant was eliminated. The regulatory committee procedure was simplified. The Parliament was not altogether satisfied with what it had obtained in supervising implementing powers in the area of co-decision, and therefore maintained its resistance and threatened intensified conflicts in legislative procedures under co-decision. Member states finally conceded to the Parliament the right to blow the whistle if it felt that a draft implementing measure or a proposal submitted to the Council under the regulatory committee procedure was exceeding the powers conferred on the Commission in the field of co-decision.[5]

What particularly mattered to the Parliament were systematic criteria for a distinction between legislative and implementing measures, and for the choice of a given type of committee procedure. Some member states rejected this line, wishing to stick to a case-by-case procedure. The final outcome did not greatly depart from the Commission's proposal, according to which management and safeguard procedures should be reserved for 'management measures', while regulatory committees should be used for measures to apply essential provisions of basic instruments, or to update certain non-essential provisions of basic instruments. The advisory committee procedure should be applied in all situations where the management and regulatory procedure were not considered appropriate.

With the Second Comitology Decision in 1999, the Parliament's right of information was replaced by a legally binding commitment that it would receive the committee agendas for draft implementing measures

---

[5] If that was the case, the Commission would have to re-examine the measure and either submit a new draft proposal or present a proposal for normal legislation.

and the results of voting within the area of co-decision.[6] With respect to the 'whistle-blowing mechanism', it was agreed that the Parliament could object within one month after the date of receipt of the final draft of an implementing measure if it deemed that a measure exceeded the powers conferred on the Commission.

What emerges as the most salient factor of change in this period is the reinforced *bargaining power* of the Parliament. This increased bargaining power is reflected in institutional changes favouring the Parliament. The Parliament's bargaining power is used on a twofold basis: its formal power under co-decision; and its budgetary control. By skilfully linking the power in each of the arenas (co-decision and budget control) to the arena where the new comitology rules were negotiated, the Parliament was able to increase its influence in the latter, even if formally it merely had a consultative role. By threatening 'inter-institutional conflicts' and by stalling the legislative process, it obtained a formalized *droit de regard* and a right of whistle blowing, thereby supporting our *H2*.

At the beginning of the subsequent period from the *Second Comitology Decision (1999)* to the *Nice Treaty* and the *Lamfalussy Reform (2001)*, institutional questions became ever more pressing in view of the imminent (10-member state) enlargement round. With more numerous and diverse member state interests, it was expected that decision making would be more difficult, even under QMV, and presumably more delegation through decision making in comitology would become necessary. A significant institutional innovation of delegated decision making that occurred in the context of the Lamfalussy Reform was meant to enable speedy adoption of legislation within the field of financial securities markets. New framework legislation was to be adopted that would be linked to a delegation of powers to the Commission, subject to comitology under the regulatory procedure and an enhanced consultation of market actors. The Parliament stated its concern and asked for a call-back right if dissatisfied with the delegation.

Only after a year of negotiations was a compromise reached: the Commission accepted that the Parliament should have three months instead of one to examine draft implementing measures, and not just with respect to scope but also as to substance. The Commission also promised to include a 'sunset clause' in the proposal for framework legislation of financial markets regulation, fixing a specific date at which delegation would automatically expire. The compromise reflected the Parliament's willingness to accept delegation and comitology for pragmatic reasons,

---

[6] It was also granted a summary record of meetings and a list of the authorities and organizations to which the committee members belonged.

but only if, in return, it would be granted a real power to exercise its responsibility for political supervision. In sum, by using its power under co-decision, the Parliament was able to influence the framework directive defining the Lamfalussy Reform, and secured the inclusion of a sunset clause allowing for the reconsideration of the entire framework after a certain period of time, confirming our expectations under *H2*. As we will see, the sunset clause in 2005 served the Parliament as a lever to press for a reform of the Second Comitology Decision; and indeed as a lever for the changes made in favour of the Parliament under the Lisbon Treaty.

In the following period from the Lamfalussy Reform (2001) to the Convention (2003), and from the IGC (2004) to the Third Comitology Decision (2006), given the extensive round of Eastern enlargement, the call for further institutional reforms had by no means abated, but evolved at three different levels: the Commission White Paper on Governance; the proposal for reform of the Second Comitology Decision; and the European Convention. The Commission, in its White Paper on Governance, called for a reform of its implementing powers along the model previously proposed. Legislation should be reduced to essential principles and framework legislation called 'laws', and should be adopted jointly by the Council and the Parliament. The regulations or decisions necessary to implement legislation would be adopted by the Commission, subject to supervision by the Council and the Parliament by means of a 'call-back' system.

At another level, attempts were made to reform the Second Comitology Decision of 1999. The Commission's proposal basically sought to transform comitology from an arena of member states participating in the exercise of implementing powers into an arena for the 'legislature' (Council and Parliament) supervising the 'executive' (the Commission), whose autonomy was to be strengthened (House of Lords Select Committee 31st Report 1.7.2003). More specifically, the Commission proposed to more rigorously define the criteria for the choice of committee procedure; the regulatory committee should be used whenever executive measures were designed to implement essential aspects of the basic instruments, i.e. laws, or to adapt certain aspects of them; the advisory committee procedure was to be used when the executive measure had an individual, limited scope. The new regulatory committee procedure would have two phases: the 'executive phase' would be the same as under the Second Comitology Decision of 1999, the only difference being that, in the case of an unfavourable opinion or no opinion from the committee, the Commission would not have to submit a proposal to the Council; during one further month the committee, voting by QMV, should make another attempt to come to a solution. In the 'supervisory' phase, the final draft would be submitted to the Parliament and the Council. If objections were raised,[7] the Commission would be left with two options: either to enact the measure, possibly amending its draft to take account of the objections; or to present a legislative proposal under the co-decision procedure.[8]

The Commission submitted this proposal to the Council. One month later, the Parliament initiated the consultation process and immediately rejected the provision that the Commission *could*, but *did not have to* take into account the amendments of the Parliament and the Council. The Commission was not willing to yield on the regulatory committee procedure and the Parliament refused to accept that the Commission was free to adopt an implementing measure even if it was not in line with the views of the legislator. However, somewhat surprisingly it then accepted the Commission's proposal, probably because it placed all its hopes on the imminent Convention on the Future of Europe (the Convention). The revised Commission proposal stated that, in the case of the Parliament and the Council objecting to a draft measure, the Commission could choose between (i) a modification of the draft; (ii) the presentation of a legislative proposal; (iii) the adoption of the draft without change; (iv) the withdrawal of the draft measure (Commission proposal of April 2004). This proposal, however, was removed from public attention due to the European Convention, which opened a phase of fundamental reform of the comitology system.

In the Convention, which to an important extent consisted of members of national parliaments and members of the European Parliament, parliamentary influence was significant. The working group chaired by Giuliano Amato proposed a classification of legal instruments that would be clear to the European public: basic laws should be called 'framework laws' and 'laws', while regulations and decisions should be (non-legislative) implementing acts. It also proposed a hierarchy of legal acts: legislative acts, called laws and framework laws; and non-legislative acts, i.e. ('delegated acts') and implementing acts taking the form of regulations and decisions. While the working group had proposed that implementing decisions would be the only acts in which comitology would continue to apply, the Praesidium insisted that comitology would have to take into account the fact that the Council was no

---

[7] With absolute majority in the Parliament and QMV in the Council within one month, which could be extended to two months.

[8] Moreover, the existing provision allowing the Parliament an *ultra vires* statement, i.e. a statement that a measure which exceeded the Commission's implementing powers should be abolished because the new provision would allow the Parliament to object to both the scope and substance of a draft implementing measure under co-decision.

longer the only legislator. Therefore, the procedure for defining the principles and rules of comitology should be shifted to co-decisions.

In plenary discussion, the Chair of the Praesidium noted that there was broad agreement to adopt a hierarchy of legal acts and a distinction between legislative and non-legislative acts. At the same time, however, diverging views on details were expressed, many of them relating to delegated regulations. Nevertheless, only some of the amendments induced the Praesidium to incorporate changes into its original draft which was adopted by the plenary in June 2003 (Héritier 2007). The text provided that legislative acts would have the form of laws or framework laws, while non-legislative acts would take the form of regulations or decisions. To control the executive there would be (1) a mechanism of control on a case-by-case basis through a right of call-back, i.e. to retrieve the right to legislate by the Council or Parliament; (2) a period of tacit approval: if the Council and the Parliament raised no objections, Delegated Acts would enter into force; and (3) a sunset clause: Delegated Acts would have a limited period of duration which could be extended by the Parliament *and* the Council (Christiansen and Vaccari 2009: 339).

During the IGC, the hierarchy of legal acts as proposed by the Convention was not taken up and renegotiated. The final version stated in Article I-36 of the Constitutional Treaty that, where uniform conditions for implementing legally binding Union acts are needed, European laws and framework laws may delegate to the Commission the power to adopt delegated European regulations to supplement or amend non-essential elements of the laws and framework laws, or in duly justified cases to the Council (Article I-40 CT). The essential elements are reserved to laws and framework laws. European laws and framework laws would lay down the conditions to which delegation is subject, conditions that would include the Council's and Parliament's right to revoke the delegation. The delegation regulation could enter into force only if no objection had been expressed by the Parliament or the Council within a period set by law. For this purpose, European laws would lay down in advance the rules and general principles of controlling the Commission's implementing powers (Christiansen and Vaccari 2009: 339).

Since the process of ratification of the Constitutional Treaty came to a sudden halt in 2005, the revision of the Second Comitology Decision moved back to centre stage. The Parliament decided to refuse the renewal of the Lamfalussy framework legislation under the sunset clause, and proceeded to block individual items under the Lamfalussy system. It also withheld part of the budget for committees (Interview, EP, February 2006). These three measures boosted its indirect influence on the revision of the Comitology Decision, a decision in which the

Parliament did not formally take part other than being consulted. The Commission resubmitted its proposal (of 2002) which had sought to redefine the logic of comitology from being a national input into the exercise of implementing powers, to being supervision by the 'legislature' over the 'executive', and in line with that, to strengthen the autonomy of the Commission. But according to the Commission itself, the main objective of its proposal was to

> take account of the European Parliament's position as a co-legislator... placing on an equal footing the European Parliament and the Council as supervisors of the Commission's exercise of the implementing powers. (Explanatory Memorandum for Commission Proposal of 11.12.2002)[9]

The central features of the proposal consisted of defining criteria for the choice of committee procedure and a reform of the regulatory committee procedure which would provide the two arms of 'the legislature' with equal opportunities to exercise control. The exercise of implementing powers would be split into two parallel regimes: one for matters falling outside co-decision and another for matters falling inside. This is indeed what the Parliament had always been asking for since the introduction of the co-decision procedure. But the envisaged reform of the regulatory committee procedure would open up a new possibility for the Commission itself to adopt implementing measures regardless of objections from either the Council or the Parliament. The Council would no longer be permitted to prevent a proposal from being adopted (the *contre-filet* mechanism) (Commission Draft November 2005). As noted by the then British Minister for Europe, Denis McShane, the Commission had tried in the past to 'secure this licence', but the Council always resisted (House of Lords Select Committee on the EU, 22.3.2004: 20/21).

The Council, although aware that some sort of reform had to be undertaken to please the Parliament and to 'buy' support for another period of the Lamfalussy system, was rather sceptical with respect to the Commission's intentions. There was close to unanimous agreement in the Council that there should only be a limited reform focused on regulatory committees and on the question of normative quality. In particular, the Council emphasized the need to meet the Parliament's wishes to define criteria to delimit the scope for implementing measures of 'legislative' or 'quasi-legislative' quality, but at the same time it sought to preserve room for manoeuvre for itself. It was willing to concede in the case of quasi-legislative decisions (which did not concern purely executive decisions) that the Parliament (and the Council) should be

---

[9] Proposal for a Council Decision amending Decision 99/468/EC.

granted more competences to block a decision or to exercise some ex post opportunity for control (Interview, the Council, February 2006), extending the period from one to three month(s).[10]

But the Council was profoundly unwilling to extend the Parliament's right to review matters dealt with under the regulatory committee procedure from procedural matters to substantive fields (Interview, the Council, February 2006). Support for this position is found in an opinion of its Legal Service which reasserted the Council's Treaty-based right to exercise delegated 'executive' functions and not merely 'legislative' functions (thus contesting the 'separation of powers' logic of the Parliament and the Commission). Importantly, the Parliament has no corresponding right (Interview, the Council, February 2006).[11] The proposal to enable MEPs to attend committee meetings was also rejected.

The Parliament, in response—besides using the Lamfalussy lever—also launched an offensive by systematically introducing amendments to restrict the scope of delegation (Corbett 1998: 258; Bergström et al. 2007), as illustrated in Figure 3.1. It presents the type of modifications that the Parliament (and the Council) inserted in the Commission's delegation proposals.

It shows that the Parliament—while rarely rejecting delegation entirely—restricted its scope much more frequently under co-decision than it did under cooperation. Under cooperation procedure, the Parliament either rejected delegation or reduced the substantive extent of delegation as proposed by the Commission in one-third of the cases. By contrast, it has done so in almost 70 per cent of cases under the co-decision procedure. It appears, therefore, that the Parliament does not oppose delegation altogether, even if it technically could have done so under co-decision procedure, but rather opposes delegation of *large scope*.

In short, the outcome of the Parliament's successful bargaining for power is that it has become an almost co-equal player with the Council in the context of delegation under the Lisbon Treaty. An important lever used by the Parliament to achieve this outcome was—in accordance with the above cross-arena linkage argument—to threaten not to extend the Lamfalussy system of financial market regulation if the member state governments failed to give new delegation powers to the Parliament. The success of this strategy is reflected in the fact that the

[10] The Council arguably asked the President of the Parliament for a commitment in return for any concessions, such as a statement to the effect that 'we have now ended the conflict over comitology' (Interview, the Council, February 2006).

[11] Article 202 EC excluded a delegation of executive powers to the Parliament.

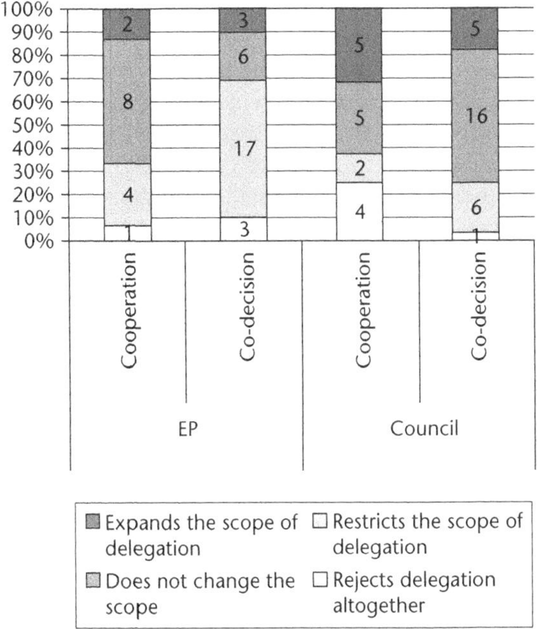

Figure 3.1 The EP's and the Council's modification of the Commission's delegation proposals, per type of procedure in use, N = 44 Art. 130s(1)

Parliament was able to secure a regulatory procedure with scrutiny, which granted to both legislators the competence to block in 2006 a Commission decision (Bergström and Héritier 2007; Bergström et al. 2007).

In the negotiation of the Lisbon Treaty it was an important concern of the Council and its Legal Service and the Commission—by revising the Treaty—to make legislation and delegation more efficient. The concern of rendering legislation more efficient is also frequently stated in Presidency Conclusions. The intellectual foundations were laid in the Final Report of Working Group IX on Simplification in the Convention (Amato's working group) (see Section 3.2). The provisions of the Lisbon Treaty are more or less identical to those envisaged by that Working Group.

> [T]he Group proposes a new type of 'delegated' act which, accompanied by strong control mechanisms, could encourage the legislator to look solely to the essential elements of an act and to delegate the more technical aspects to the executive, provided that it had the guarantee that it would be able to retrieve, as it were, its power to legislate. (Report Working Group pp. 8–9)

For the first time the notion of 'legislation' (and of 'non-legislation') was introduced into the Treaty text and the role of the Council and the Parliament are characterized as the roles of the 'legislator'.

The member states took pains to ensure that the provisions on delegation introduced by the Lisbon Treaty (Art. 290 TFEU) would not become a reason for the Commission to discontinue its consultation of national experts within the Lamfalussy system.[12] For this reason a Declaration was attached to the Treaty in which the member state governments emphasize their expectation that the Commission will 'continue to consult experts appointed by the Member States in the preparation of draft "delegated acts" in the financial services area, in accordance with its established practice'.[13] As a Declaration, it has no legally binding effect, but it is nevertheless politically 'binding'.

This concern for efficiency and concern for the Lamfalussy system made the Council and the Commission vulnerable to the Parliament's attempts to link substantive legislative issues under co-decision to issues of institutional design. Because the Council and the Commission were keen 'to get things done', they have yielded to the demands of the Parliament for more institutional power. The choice was between on the one hand including the Parliament in order to achieve more; and on the other hand resisting the Parliament's offensive and facing the consequences: obstructionism and delay in linked arenas. Indeed the entire driving force behind concessions to the Parliament with respect to comitology arrangements may be seen as that of unblocking the process and releasing its full potential.

3.3 Conclusion

This chapter has traced the changes of the institutional rules governing comitology from the perspective of the role that the Parliament played in this contest for power in shaping these rules. We based our analysis on the assumption that institutional rules are incomplete contracts that leave room for renegotiation as they are applied in day-to-day practice

---

[12] While the level three process was invented by the Lamfalussy system itself, the other major component, the comitology aspects following the CAP and foodstuffs regulation, were imposed by the Commission and accepted by member-state governments. The models used for the design of the Lamfalussy system, in turn, were the decision-making procedures in agricultural policy and consumer protection.

[13] 'The Conference takes note of the Commission's intention to continue to consult experts appointed by the Member States in the preparation of draft delegated acts in the financial services area, in accordance with its established practice' (Declaration (39) on Art. 290 TFEU).

and that the outcome of these renegotiations, leading to informal insti-tutional rules in the application of formal rules, reflects the relative power of the actors involved. The relative power of the negotiating actors derives from the availability of a fall-back position in case negoti-ations fail. We further assumed that there are multiple decision-making arenas, and we distinguished rule-designing actors A in rule-designing arena A from substantive legislative decision-makers B deciding in a substantive policy arena B. While actors A have formal decision-making powers in *both* arenas and thereby form a link between the two arenas, actors B only have decision-making powers in arena B. We argue that actors in arena B—who have no formal say in arena A—by withholding their support for a decision in arena B, indirectly influence institutional decisions taken in arena A (pressure to which actors A are susceptible because they are actors in both arenas).

Applied to the Parliament, we argue that, when the Parliament puts pressure on both the Commission and the Council, and threatens to withhold its support for a substantive legislative matter in the co-deci-sion and/or budgetary arenas B, it can indirectly influence the shaping of comitology rules in arena A. We contend that this has been the main driver of change in the shaping of comitology rules, which has resulted in a substantial increase in the Parliament's influence in delegation. Moreover, we also show that actors may turn to third-party dispute resolution in the hope of settling in their favour a conflict about rule application. However, since the outcome of a third-party ruling is uncer-tain (the preferences of the conflict ruling actors, i.e. courts, cannot be assumed ex ante), relying on third-party dispute settlement to strengthen one's own position may just be a 'shot in the dark' which may or may not work. By empirically investigating the role of the Parliament in the development of comitology rules over time, we carried out a plausibility scrutiny of this argument. Distinguishing different periods under which comitology rules underwent clear changes, and applying a backward-looking design, we empirically scrutinized how the Parliament had been affected; and then proceeded to identify the rele-vant factors accounting for the outcome. We did indeed find considerable evidence of the Parliament successfully applying cross-arena pressure in order to strengthen its institutional role in comitology, thus advancing it from a position in which it was only a marginal player in comitology to a position of strength almost equal to that of the Council.

4

Delegation under the Lisbon Treaty

The Treaty on the Functioning of the European Union[1] (TFEU) breaks new ground. It distinguishes for the first time between legislative delegation and executive delegation, and provides for two separate procedures for Delegated Acts and implementing acts (Ponzan-o 2010). Under Delegated Acts (Art. 290 TFEU), the Commission—by legislation—may be delegated the power to adopt acts of general scope, supplementing or amending certain non-essential elements of the legislation in question. The legislators must explicitly define the objective, content, scope, and duration of this delegation. They can also choose mechanism(s) to control the Commission when it applies these delegated powers.

The Treaty mentions two examples of such mechanisms, revocation and objection. In the case of revocation, no agreement of the Council and the Parliament is necessary to revoke a delegation. Objection by the Council or the Parliament within a period defined in the basic act is a second possible instrument. An objection on the part of either the Council or the Parliament would prevent an individual Delegated Act from coming into force. At the same time, the old comitology procedures, i.e. regulatory, advisory, and management committees, were abolished (see also Blom-Hansen 2011a, b).

In negotiating the details of *Delegated Acts* (Art. 290 TFEU) the Parliament in its Draft Report on the power of legislative delegation (2010/2021(INI)) emphasized the need for early consultation with the Commission, and the continuous transmission of information and relevant documents to the Parliament's responsible committees in the preparatory stage of Delegated Acts. It also underlines the need for an early

---

[1] The Treaty on the functioning of the European Union is the new version of the pre-existing Treaty of the European Community which resulted from the numerous amendments made through the Lisbon Treaty. It entered into force in 1 December 2009.

exchange of information with the Council and the Commission before revocation is discussed.

The Report disapproves of the Commission's tendency to treat Delegated Acts 'as though they were based on Art. 202 TEC' (Report on the Power of Delegated Legislation 2010/2021((INI), p. 10). It is particularly critical of the Member States' intention to establish committees composed of experts from the Member States which—in its view—'have no role to play in this area' (Draft Report on the Power of Delegated Legislation 2010/2021((INI), p. 11). Rather, it strongly underlines that the Commission should informally consult civil society, interest representatives, companies, social partners, and academics when drafting a decision. It also invites the Commission to involve the responsible organs of the Parliament in the preparations leading up to the adoption of Delegated Acts.

In clear contradiction to this, the Mertens Report of the Council of December 2009 called for just the opposite: the insertion of a provision in the Commission Communication:

> that there will be a systematic consultation of experts…which will be composed of experts from the authorities that are responsible for implementation of the relevant legislation in all 27 Member States, [and that] the groups will be given sufficient time to enable them to fully contribute their expertise [and] that at the end of the process the Commission chair will sum up the main elements brought forward by the experts, give a preliminary reaction and indicate how the Commission intends to proceed. (Mertens Report 16998/09: 3)

These provisions would be crucial if national delegations were to accept the proposal of the Commission Communication (see also UK House of Commons EU Scrutiny Committee of 13 July 2011 [paragraph 10.4]).

In more detail, Delegated Acts under Art. 290 TFEU do not constitute a new type of decision making. The article identifies instead a segment of all that was previously encompassed by a wide notion of 'implementation' (cf. Art. 202 TEC) and introduces a new logic for that segment. Instead of the logic of 'implementation' in the new, more narrow sense (Art. 291 TFEU), which is bottom–up (Member States vis-à-vis Commission), the logic of 'delegation' (Art. 290 TFEU) is top–down (EU legislators vis-à-vis EU executive). Studying the category of Delegated Acts, the aforementioned distinction must be kept in mind between the two functions or stages of 'comitology' (as we know it from before): the control at the stage of formal decision making; and cooperation and coordination at a preparatory stage. A central question in both these functions relates to the actors who are in the working of the committees, and the extent to which they should be regarded as 'experts' or 'representatives'. The power given to these actors, as described above, is arguably what the conflict and ensuing negotiations between Council/ Member States, the Commission, and the EP was all about.

When analysing the new Delegated Acts (Art. 290 TFEU), we may ask (1) what happens to control at the stage of formal decision making? and (2) what happens with cooperation and coordination at the preparatory stage? As regards the first question, the wording of Art. 290 TFEU clearly indicates that control will be in the hands of the Council and the Parliament. Legislative acts shall explicitly lay down the conditions to which the delegation is subject; these conditions may be as follows: the Parliament or the Council may decide to revoke the delegation, i.e. the Delegated Act may come into force only if no objections have been expressed by the Parliament or the Council within a period set by the legislative act. Hence, Art. 290 TFEU allows the legislator, in delegating legislation, to require that the Commission may only begin to exercise a delegated competence if certain objective legal or factual preconditions are at hand. It does now allow a requirement to be made that the Commission must involve any institution or body that acts in accordance with the comitology model (defined as procedures of control by committee). Art. 290 TFEU, however, allows the legislator to provide that the Commission shall consult 'experts' during the preparatory phase of the Delegated Acts as long as this does not constitute a mandatory part of the Delegated Act, and that the result of such consultation is not binding on the Commission. In other words, it may not be required that 'representatives' exercise control over the Commission at the stage of formal decision making, but it may still be expected and to some extent compelled (although not legally) to consult 'experts' to ensure cooperation and coordination at a preparatory stage.

What happens with the second function of comitology, i.e. cooperation and coordination at a preparatory stage in delegating legislation? First, in accordance with the conclusions above, it may be required, in delegating legislation, that the Commission shall consult 'experts' during the preparatory phase of the Delegated Acts (as long as this does not constitute a mandatory part of the Delegated Act and that the results of such consultation are not binding on the Commission). Second, there may be good reasons for the Commission to seek cooperation and coordination at a preparatory stage. Hence, as indicated above, the question is what 'experts' really means and who gets to decide?

This is dealt with in particular by the so-called Common Understanding signed up to by the Council, the Commission, and the Parliament. The Common Understanding is not by its very nature a legally binding document and can therefore not 'enter into effect'; but for all practical purposes it would seem that the date closest to that was 11 April 2011.

> The Common Understanding is an agreement between the three EU institutions that sets out the practical arrangements, definitions and preferences relating to delegations of legislative power to the Commission under Art. 290 TFEU. It is a formal agreement that all three institutions shall cooperate to ensure the Council and Parliament have 'effective control' of the Commission's exercise of these delegated powers and it is hoped, will facilitate a smoother passage for this form of legislation through the EU machine. The Parliament agreed upon the text of the Common Understanding on 3 April 2011. It was then communicated to the Council, and therefore Member States, on 4 April 2011. The Common Understanding was adopted at COREPER I on 15 April 2011. (UK House of Commons EU Scrutiny Committee 13 July 2011 [paragraph 10:1])[2]

The Common Understanding states that the Commission is to consult national experts based on the Commission Communication of 2009. To solve the conflict with the Parliament about the inclusion of national experts described above, the Council dropped its insistence in the Common Understanding on national experts from responsible national authorities, and in return obtained reference to the Commission Communication of 2009, which in turn refers to national experts from responsible national authorities. While this is not a legal obligation for the Commission it nonetheless constitutes commitment on the part of the Commission, well knowing that if it did not live up to expectation, the Council would not delegate.

Of particular interest for us are paragraphs 1 and 4:

> 'Taking into account the commitments mentioned by the Commission in the communication of 9 December 2009, this Common Understanding builds further on that communication and streamlines the practice established thereafter by the EP and the Council. It sets out the practical arrangements and agreed clarifications and preferences applicable to delegations of legislative power under Art. 290 of the TFEU, in accordance with the objectives, content, scope and duration of a delegation, which must be expressly defined in each legislative act making a delegation...' (paragraph 1). 'The Commission, when preparing and drawing up delegated acts, will ensure a simultaneous, timely and appropriate transmission of relevant documents to the EP and the Council and carry out appropriate and transparent consultations well in advance, including at expert level. The EP and the Council shall indicate to the Commission their respective functional mailbox to be

---

[2] The Common Understanding is not formally published and the most official reference to it appears to be: Council of the EU; Brussels 10 April 2011, Note from the Presidency to Delegations: Common Understanding—Delegated Acts (8753/11).

used for the transmission of documents relating to these consultations.'
(paragraph 4)

The Common Understanding should hence be read in conjunction with
the earlier—explicitly mentioned and underlying—Commission Communication of 9 December 2009. More specifically, the Commission
explicitly commits itself:[3]

> to carry out the preparatory work it considers necessary in order to ensure,
> first, that from a technical and legal point of view the delegated acts comply
> fully with the objectives laid down by the basic instrument and, second, that
> from a political and institutional point of view everything possible is done to
> avoid any objections being made by Parliament or the Council. Except in cases
> where this preparatory work does not require any new expertise, *the Commis-*
> *sion intends systematically to consult experts from the national authorities of all the*
> *Member States, which will be responsible for implementing the delegated acts once*
> *they have been adopted* (emphasis added). This consultation will be carried out
> in plenty of time, to give the experts an opportunity to make a useful and
> effective contribution to the Commission. The Commission might form new
> expert groups for this purpose, or use existing ones. The Commission attaches
> the highest importance to this work, which makes it possible to establish an
> effective partnership at the technical level with experts in the national author-
> ities. However, it should be made clear that *these experts will have a consultative*
> *rather than an institutional role in the decision-making procedure* (emphasis
> added). At the end of the consultations, the Commission will inform the
> experts of the conclusions it believes should be drawn from the discussions,
> its preliminary reactions and how it intends to proceed.

The UK House of Commons EU Scrutiny Committee of 13 July 2011
points out that the Common Understanding is an improvement on the
Commission's 2009 Communication: Although the Commission has no
legal obligation to consult Member States, the Council, or the Parliament before adopting Delegated Acts, it has committed itself 'to carrying out appropriate and transparent consultations well in advance'. In
addition, member states have also secured a strong commitment by the
Commission to consult member states at expert level. 'This gives
Member States the opportunity to influence the content of "delegated
acts" and ensures that the Council will be better placed to decide
whether to exercise its powers of revocation and objection' (UK House
of Commons EU Scrutiny Committee of 13 July 2011, paragraph 10.8).
In short, the fact that the Commission intends to systematically
consult experts from the national authorities of all Member States,

---

[3] Communication from the Commission, the EP, and the Council, Brussels 9 December
2009, Implementation of Article 290 of the TFEU COM (2009) 673 final.

who will be responsible for implementing the Delegated Acts once they have been adopted, will help the Council to decide whether to exercise its powers of revocation and objection. The Council also 'notes with satisfaction the Commission's commitment to inform the experts of the conclusions it believes would be drawn from the discussions, its preliminary reactions and how it intends to proceed . . . ' and emphasizes that

> the Council draws the Commission's attention to the fundamental importance of the immediate implementation of the above mentioned commitments in order to create confidence in the new procedure foreseen under Art. 290 of the TFEU and to ensure a smooth and fruitful operation of the delegation of powers.

Moreover, it emphasizes that the 'Council intends to assess how efficiently the consultation of experts is functioning'.[4] A standard reference of 'consultation of experts at the preparatory stage' is made in the narrative. Hence pressure is used to induce the Commission to include experts.

We may conclude that this Council statement clearly manifests the political conditions underlying the Commission Communication and indeed the Common Understanding which may be summarized as 'if the Commission will not play by these rules, there will be no delegation'.

But what about the Parliament under the new Delegated Acts (Art. 290)? The Parliament, in the Framework Agreement of 20 October 2010 on the relations between the Parliament and the Commission, is guaranteed that the Commission will provide full information and documentation on its meetings with national experts within the framework of its work on the preparation and implementation of Union legislation. If so requested by the Parliament, the Commission may also invite Parliament's experts to attend those meetings. If invited at an early point in time to the consultation of experts, representatives of the Parliament may use the information collected in these early discussions in the further rounds of decision making (Interview, EP, January 2012).

As regards *implementing acts* (Art. 291), the new comitology regulation of February 2011 adopted by the Council and the Parliament specifies its implementation. It brought a shift from Decision to Regulation denoting that the legal effects are not, as they were before, limited to the 'addressees' in a narrow sense (most certainly Commission, Council,

---

[4] Council of the EU, Brussels 14 December 2009, Note from COREPER to Council, Commission Communication on Article 290 of the TFEU COM (2009) 673 final—Approval by the Council (17512/09 LIMITE).

and EP). Rather, a Regulation has general application and in its entirety is binding on, and directly applicable to, all Member States. Compared to the old Decision adopted by the Council alone, the new Regulation has been adopted by the Council and Parliament jointly in an ordinary legislative procedure. The new Regulation emphasizes that 'implementation' is a responsibility of Member States and that the control exercised by the committees is such that it ensures that the Commission can be 'subject to the control of Member States' (rather than control by Council). As before, committees are composed of 'representatives of the Member States' (Art. 3 of the Regulation).

It leaves the basic system of committees, but changes the procedures guiding the work in the committees and the controls over the Commission. It distinguishes between the advisory procedure and the examination procedure. Under the advisory procedure the committee delivers its opinion. If necessary, a vote is taken under simple majority of the component members. The Commission decides, 'taking the utmost account of the conclusions drawn from the discussions within the committee' (Regulation No. 182/2011, 16.2.2011, Art. 4). The advisory procedure would be the general rule to be applied for all policy domains and all types of binding implementation decisions.

The regulation also introduces a new *examination procedure* which replaces the existing management and regulatory committees. It applies to implementing measures of general scope, programmes with 'substantial implications', measures relating to CAP and fisheries, the environment, security and safety, protection of health and safety of humans, animals and plants, taxation, and Common Commercial Policy. The Council and the Parliament—following specified guidelines—decide what measures are subject to the examination procedure. The examination procedure provides for two stages: if in the first stage (the member state committee), the national representatives vote by QMV in favour of the Commission proposal, the latter is adopted. If not, the proposal is referred to the Appeal Committee, the second possible stage. It consists of member state representatives and is chaired by the Commission. Member states can propose amendments to the proposal that the Commission may (but is not required to) include.

Member states may block a Commission decision by QMV. This also holds for most matters falling within the Common Commercial Policy (with the exception of specific multilateral safeguard measures requiring support under QMV and a transitional agreement which permits the Appeal Committee to block the adoption of a definitive anti-dumping measure by simple majority for a period of eighteen months (Regulation No. 182/ 2011, 16.2.2011). The pre-existing mechanisms for referral of disagreements have been transferred from a committee of the Council to an 'appeal committee' consisting of representatives of member states governments at a sufficiently high level (Rules of Procedure for the appeal committee, 29.3.2011; Arts 1.5 and 3.7 Comitology Regulation).[5] The role of the Parliament may be weaker than before: the new or at least enhanced logic that the control exercised by committees is the 'control of Member states' is a fundamental objection against any argument that the Parliament or indeed the Council should have a role within committees, since they are external to the system (being two arms of the EU legislator). At the same time, this means no real loss for the members of the Council since they reappear in their guise of 'Member States'. Hence it is not surprising that the Council—if confronted with a choice—tends to favour implementing acts (Art. 291) over Delegated Acts (Art. 290).

The information to be provided to the Parliament on the work of comitology committees is defined in the Council Decision of 28 June 1999, the inter-institutional agreement of 3 June 2008 between the Parliament and the Commission on comitology procedures, and instruments necessary for the implementation of Art. 291 TFEU. The Parliament does not have right of access to full information and documentation on the Commission's meetings with national experts in comitology committees (Framework Agreement 20 October 2010, Annex 1 [2]).

Looking at the practical use of delegated or implementing acts under Arts 290 and 291 in quantitative terms, it emerges that in the regulations and directives of 2010 and 2011, Delegated Acts (Art. 290) as opposed to implementing acts (Art. 291) have only been used very marginally.[6] Of the sixty-six directives adopted by the Commission in

---

[5] The member states 'may make suggestions on this regard and indicate the level of representation that they consider appropriate which should be of a sufficiently high and horizontal nature, including at Ministerial level. As a general rule, representation should not be below the level of member of the committee of Permanent Representatives of the governments of the Member States. The Commission shall take the utmost account of such suggestions' (Rules of Procedure for the appeal committee, 29.3.2011; Art. 1.5 and Art. 3.7 Comitology Regulation).

[6] A piece of legislation typically includes a delegation clause (Art. 290), but also a 'comitology' clause (Art. 291). A typical delegation clause in the *Preamble* would state 'the power to adopt acts in accordance with Art. 290 of the TFEU should be delegated to the Commission in respect of... It is of particular importance that the Commission carry out appropriate consultations during its preparatory work, including at expert level. The Commission, when preparing and drawing up delegated acts, should ensure a simultaneous, timely and appropriate transmission of relevant documents to the EP and the Council'. In the main text in a typical delegation clause there is no mention of the preparatory stage or experts, stating 'The delegation of power... shall be conferred on the Commission for a period of five years... The Commission shall draw up a report in the respect of the delegation of the power not later than nine months before the end of the five-year period. The delegation of power shall be tacitly extended for periods of an identical duration, unless the EP or the Council opposes in

2010, none was a Delegated Act (Art. 290); all sixty-six were implementing acts (Art. 291). Of the 589 regulations adopted by the Commission in 2010, four were Delegated Acts (Art. 290) and 585 were implementing acts (Art. 291). In 2011 (up to 7 December 2011) there were about[7] 600 Commission regulations which are *not* referred to as 'delegated acts' (Art. 290), and thus must be considered as implementing acts (Art. 291). There are seventy-two Commission directives *not* referred to as 'delegated', and thus according to the post-Lisbon nomenclature must be considered as 'implementing' acts.[8]

It is noteworthy that a relatively high number of delegations (Art. 290) have been made in legislation adopted in 2010 and 2011 which have *not yet* resulted in Delegated Acts. Hence the Council allowed for delegation in the last two years by introducing delegation clauses in legislation, although the Commission has not yet followed these up. The reasons may be that the detailed rules in the Common Understanding about how to apply Art. 290 had first to be negotiated. It is plausible that the actors involved hesitated to use the decision mechanism because it was not clear how the power distribution between the actors would be implemented after negotiation of the specifics of Art. 290. Legislation under co-decision—but not Council legislation—fell drastically in 2010, while there was uncertainty as regards the division of competences between Council and Parliament regarding Art. 290; this should be resolved with the adoption of the Common Understanding.[9] Hence almost everything is still about 'comitology' in the classic sense (Art. 291). From the viewpoint of the Parliament, when the Council tries to avoid Delegated Acts, it goes if at all possible for implementing acts, or alternatively legislation. Under both, its formal rights of cooperation and coordination as well as control are guaranteed (Interview, EP, January 2012).

First of all, the Commission has to present a convincing argument to the legislator demonstrating why it wants the power to adopt a

---

such extension not later than three months before the end of each period . . . The delegation of power referred to . . . may be revoked at any time by the EP or by the Council. A decision to revoke shall put an end to the delegation of power specified in that decision . . .' (see e.g. Dir. 2011/82/EU of the EP and of the Council of 25 October 2011 facilitating the cross-border exchange of information on road safety related to traffic offences [OJ 2011 L 288/1]).

[7] It may be that fewer than 100 per cent of all temporary regulations within the daily management of CAP and published in the Official Journal (OJ) in light type were excluded.

[8] Own calculation on the basis of publication in the Official Journal 2010 and 2011. Typically a piece of legislation including a delegation clause (Art. 290) also includes a 'comitology' clause (Art. 291).

[9] A similar phenomenon could be observed in 1994 after the coming into force of the Maastricht Treaty, where there was a great deal of uncertainty as to how the new co-decision procedure would be applied.

Delegated Act.[10] As a rule, when the Commission proposes a Delegated Act, conflict ensues between the Parliament, the Council, and the Commission. The Council seeks to oppose it entirely or to reduce its scope, or to translate it into an implementing act. Frequently, in order to come to an agreement, deals are struck across various issues as to whether to use 'delegating' or implementing acts (Interview, the Commission, January 2012).

There are instances in recent legislation of such conflicts over the choice of either Art. 290 or Art. 291.[11] One instance is conflict in the case of the adoption of the Regulation on the prevention and correction of macroeconomic imbalances.[12] When deciding how to flesh out the scoreboard, i.e. the indicators used to measure and monitor macroeconomic and macro-financial imbalances, the Commission and the Parliament favoured Delegated Acts (Art. 290), while the Council wished to use an implementing act (Art. 291). A deadlock ensued which, after a round of negotiations, led to the use of a new informal type of procedure which is *neither* Art. 290 nor Art. 291, but is a 'compromise'. The respective recital 12 of the Regulation says:

> The Commission should closely cooperate with the European Parliament and the Council when drawing up the scoreboard and the set of macroeconomic and macrofinancial indicators for Member States. The Commission should present suggestions for comments to the competent committees of the European Parliament and of the Council on plans to establish and adjust the indicators and threshold. The Commission should inform the European Parliament and the Council of any changes to the indicators and threshold and explain its reasons for suggesting such changes.

Note the difference to the 'real' use of a delegation act used in another six-pack regulation on the effective enforcement of budgetary surveillance in the Euro area.[13] It states, as prescribed in the Comitology Regulation of 2010: that the Commission shall be empowered to adopt Delegated Acts regarding the criteria establishing fines, and procedures for investigations (Art. 8.4); that the Commission shall draw up a report in respect of the delegation of power; and that the delegation

---

[10] The Commission's internal guidelines to the services describe the demarcation line between Delegated Acts and implementing acts used for developing this argument.

[11] Other recent instances of a conflict between the Council, the Parliament, and the Commission about the selection of a delegated or implementing act are the Cross-Border Health Care Directive and the Novel Food Directive.

[12] Regulation (EU) No. 1176/2011 of the EP and of the Council of 16 November 2011 on the prevention and correction of macroeconomic imbalances.

[13] Regulation (EU) No. 1173/2011 of the EP and of the Council of 16 November 2011 on the effective enforcement of budgetary surveillance in the Euro area.

may be revoked at any time by the Parliament or by the Council (Arts 11.2 and 3). What is striking from our theoretical perspective of institutional change is that the existing formal rules—in the situation of a decision stalemate—were renegotiated and transformed in such a way as to overcome the impasse, but in doing so also strengthening the power of the Commission. It remains to be seen whether this informal 'compromise rule' created a precedent and will be used in other cases where there is a conflict between the bodies as to whether to use delegated or implementing acts.

The novelty under implementing acts (Art. 291) is that the Council in its entirety no longer has a role to play; but it re-enters as individual member-state representatives. From the Commission's point of view the former threat of having to go to Council in order to solve a conflict over comitology was an option to be avoided by making concessions to individual member states.[14] With the advent of the appeal committee this threat has disappeared. The Council can no longer replace the Commission (Interview, the Commission, January 2012).

Turning to the quantitative section of our analysis of delegated legislation we first give an overview of the development of legislation and delegation over time as distributed across types of legal instruments and policy areas; we then turn to the quantitative investigation of the impact of the introduction of co-decision on the Parliament's attitude towards comitology, and the impact of the Second Comitology Decision on the Commission's and the Council's preferences for the use of comitology.

---

[14] Only five to ten cases per annum went to Council for mediation of conflicts.

5

Patterns and trends in European legislation and delegation

In an attempt 'to paint the bigger picture' we present an overview of legislative and delegation activities. We describe the overall patterns and trends in legislative activity, choice of instrument, and the decision to delegate and thereby provide a backdrop for the subsequent detailed quantitative analyses. The attempt to paint the bigger picture always comes at a cost, namely, the loss of important details and distinctions. The problem of 'quantification' in studies of legal activity is essentially that laws which differ greatly in regulatory importance are implicitly equated; important developments can therefore easily drown in the ocean of aggregate numbers. However, as the analysis below will reveal, there are many interesting patterns in the composition and evolution of EU law that are relevant to the theme of this book, even if caution must be observed in drawing conclusions with respect to what the overall patterns and trends signify in substantive terms.

We will argue here that the big picture yields important insights into delegation and its use in the EU law and policy context. In our analysis we illustrate how various legal instruments are employed, and it will show how delegation occurs in different policy areas over time. This analysis requires detailed presentation of data sources and categorization which are included in Appendix 1. We will show that the strong correlation found between choice of legal instrument and the propensity to delegate provides a strong indication that there are different preferences for preserving national autonomy on the one hand and to upload competences to the supranational level on the other. These issues and tensions in the operation of the EU legislative machinery can be explored at the macro—as well as the micro—level. In this chapter we focus on the macro level, using aggregate data, whereas in the following chapters we will look more deeply into specific policy areas.

5.1 Legislative trends in European law: Instruments and quantification

European law is unique among legal orders, not only because it has such a wide range of legal instruments at its disposal, but also due to its lack of a transparent structure. Legal experts have commented on the apparent proliferation of instruments over time[1] and many have also deplored the lack of clear principles guiding their use by the European bodies. Currently, as in the past, the type of instrument itself thus reveals nothing of its origins or of its status within a hierarchy of laws that would be more familiar from national systems of law.[2] Over the years, a number of attempts have been made to remedy this situation. On the one hand, proposals aiming to simplify the system by reducing the number of instruments available have been suggested; and on the other, greater clarity has been sought by suggesting clearer definitions of the individual instruments and linking them to specific institutions (Lenaerts and Desomer 2005: 746). Most recently, as we have seen, the Lisbon Treaty did in fact introduce a distinction between legislation proper and delegating and implementing acts under delegation.

Therefore, at least until recently, the anatomy of the European legal order has presented certain practical challenges to carrying out a study of delegated legislation. In contrast to most national legal orders, one cannot infer from the type of act used the procedure used for its adoption in the EU. As two legal experts point out,

> each of the different community instruments can be used to lay down the basic policy choices in a given competence area, or, on the contrary, can contain mere technical implementation measures. In other words, the choice for a regulation, a directive, or a decision does not reveal, as such, the legislative or executive nature of the act adopted under that label. (Lenaerts and Desomer 2005: 746)

Therefore, other characteristics of the legal acts (primarily its legal basis) have to be relied on for this basic distinction, as will be discussed below.

The instruments of European law can be broadly characterized by three parameters. The first concerns the *binding versus non-binding force* of the act. Regulations, directives, and decisions are binding instruments, but

---

[1] It has been pointed out that there are about fifteen different instruments envisaged in the EU's basic Treaties and a few others have emerged outside the frameworks established by those texts (Lenaerts and Desomer 2005: 748).

[2] As von Bogdandy, Arndt, and Bast write: in continental Europe, the structures of national public law have been built on the systematization of the legal instruments available to public authorities (von Bogdandy et al. 2004).

other instruments, such as recommendations and opinions, are not. The second parameter pertains to the *scope of application* of the act. Regulations have general application in the sense that their normative scope is formulated in an abstract fashion. In contrast, directives and decisions are in principle only binding upon those to whom they are addressed. Directives and decisions can be addressed to a single member state, or to some or to all member states. Finally, decisions can also be addressed to private parties. The third parameter concerns the *type of application in member states' legal orders* and is 'therefore useful in case a uniform legal regime throughout the territory of the member states is desirable' (Lenaerts and Desomer 2005: 747).

While decisions do not require action by the nation states to take effect, directives must in principle be transposed into national law in order to have a legal bearing on individuals. Directives are therefore well suited for designing a 'mere legislative framework at the European level, while respecting the regulatory diversity in the Member States' (Lenaerts and Desomer 2005: 747). However, it should be emphasized that the sharp distinction between the instruments described here (particularly between regulations and directives) has faded somewhat in practice. Directives have become increasingly detailed in their provisions over the years and thereby effectively reduced the margin of discretion for member states. Very detailed directives thus resemble regulations in that they allow less room for differences in choice of implementing laws and impose uniformity rather than diversity of legal regime (see the Commission's White Paper on European Governance, 25 July 2001).[3]

In the present study, we are primarily interested in binding legal acts and those that ultimately have general applicability—whether in a direct sense (regulations) or indirectly through the agency of member states (directives). We have therefore decided to focus our analysis of legislative activity on regulations and directives and, in particular, the acts of delegation based on those instruments. This is not to say that decisions are not an important component of European law[4] that can be omitted without any loss. However, the dynamics of delegation where decisions constitute the main legal instrument appear to follow a different pattern, because broadly speaking the aim of decisions is not to

---

[3] A legal expert at the Commission stated that 'increasingly directives are looking like regulations in that they are so detailed that you wonder what there is left for the member states to transpose'.

[4] In purely quantitative terms regulations and decisions are the most dominant instruments of EU law. Respectively, they account for 31 and 27 per cent of the legal acts in force (see von Bogdandy et al. 2004: 98–9).

produce general law. Moreover, unlike regulations and directives, decisions are not subject to a general publication requirement. Decisions addressed to private parties can for instance be held confidentially. We consider therefore that the patterns of delegation in relation to decisions are best investigated in a separate study.[5]

What prompts the choice of regulation versus directive?

As empirical studies of the structure of EU law have shown, regulations and directives are not used to the same extent. In purely quantitative terms, regulations are clearly the dominant instrument in dynamic (acts enacted over time) as well as static (acts in force at any moment in time) terms. Moreover, as we will demonstrate in section 5.3, the usage of the two instruments varies a great deal across policy areas. There are several possible causes behind the observed variation in the use of instruments. Some treaty articles clearly stipulate what instrument should be used, but acts adopted on the basis of treaty articles that are silent on the question of instrument constitute a larger part of EU law. When this is the case, the choice of instrument falls within the jurisdiction of the EU bodies. To our knowledge, the question of what considerations prompt this choice has not been systematically explored. It is clear from other studies, however, that the choice is not random. Von Bogdandy et al. write 'closer analysis shows that institutional practice has developed legal instruments corresponding to the specific form of public authority exercised by the European Union' (von Bogdandy et al. 2004: 92).

The choice of instrument may, as Lenaerts and Desomer (2005) suggest, be due to considerations related to uniformity of legal regime versus the need for regulatory diversity in member states. The need for diversity may be interpreted at two levels. On the one hand, the use of directives may be prompted by respect for the technicalities of national legal language and the need to preserve national traditions of jurisprudence, which necessitates active translation of European rules to fit into the national body of law. On the other hand, it may equally well reflect a desire to maintain real room for political manoeuvre at the national level.

In answer to questions concerning the choice of legal instrument, an expert at the Commission largely concurred with the above-mentioned considerations. Interestingly, however, mention of legal instrument in

---

[5] Similarly, Franchino only includes regulations and directives in his study of delegation in the EU (Franchino 2007).

the relevant treaty article has not always played the determinant role in choice of instrument that might be expected. In fact, in the words of the expert, the Commission had in the past been 'a little less firm on that'. It was stressed that with the new treaty, words and deeds had been aligned, however, so a mention of legal instrument in a treaty article is interpreted as binding in terms of the choices made.[6] In this sense, the Commission enjoys less freedom of choice now than it did in the past. It should of course not be ignored that there may also in some cases be room for choice in the selection of legal base. According to the same expert, a number of other considerations play a role in the choice of instrument when the relevant treaty article is silent on the matter. First, the defining features of the regulation and directives are directly relevant. For instance, when generally binding legislation that is directly applicable to individuals is desired, the natural choice is regulation. This choice is not necessarily permanent for a given sector, as the perceived regulatory needs may change. A recent example of such changes can be found in the sector of Financial Services, which has until now been regulated mainly by directives.

Recently, however, there has been a move in this area towards thinking more of regulations, resulting from a desire to speak directly to financial institutions and to place obligations directly on them. The legal base that has been used in the past in relation to financial institutions mentions only directives, so that changing the legal instrument would in fact require changing the legal base. As the expert stated, 'it will be interesting to see if we try to shift more to an internal market legal base where you can use either a directive or a regulation'. Use of the article concerning the approximation of laws[7] was mentioned as another example of changing practices with respect to the choice of instrument. Directives have been viewed as more congruent with the aims of the article, but it has increasingly been accepted that regulations can also be used in this area and this trend may well continue.

However, changes in choice of instrument can also be prompted by more pragmatic concerns. For instance, technical standards for cars were previously in the form of a directive. However, given that there is in any

---

[6] As the expert stated: 'In the past we were perhaps a little bit less firm on that, but now with a new treaty it is quite clear that when it says directives, it means directives and when it says regulation we take it to mean regulation. There were some cases where the treaty specified an instrument and we did not quite follow that. I think there were times when it said regulation and we used directives. In the old treaty they were a little more subtle in regard to that.'

[7] Article 114 of Lisbon Treaty (Articles 95 under the Amsterdam and Nice Treaties; Article 100 in Maastricht and Rome Treaties).

case no—or very little—room for choice, member states have expressed a preference for regulation rather than a directive, so that they do not have to transpose it into national law.

Apart from congruence between the aims of the legislation and the properties of the instruments themselves, more general principles were also mentioned as important. The principles of proportionality—i.e. that the content and form of Union action shall not exceed what is necessary to achieve the objectives of the Treaties (Art. 5 of the Treaty on European Union)—and subsidiarity were also mentioned as important considerations in the choice of instrument. The choice of a directive could thus be justified by being more in line with the principle of proportionality than would be a regulation. Likewise, regulations—requiring no transposition into national law—may be more in line with the objectives of a level playing field in areas of economic competition. The prevalence of regulations in the domain of agriculture can therefore be seen as prompted by the wish to speak directly to farmers as well as to ensure identical conditions for all, thereby avoiding national differences in implementation that potentially distort competition.

LEGAL INSTRUMENT AND DELEGATION

As discussed, directives, unlike regulations, provide a framework within which the states can act independently within limits that may be widely or narrowly defined. It is therefore reasonable to expect that the choice of legal instrument ex ante (at the treaty negotiations) or ex post (in the daily functioning of the Community) is influenced by the same considerations that affect the propensity of the Council to delegate in the course of the legislative process. In fact, the application of such principles as proportionality and subsidiarity as well as uniformity and technical complexity would seem to point in this direction. Consequently, it is also highly plausible that different delegation dynamics can be observed respectively for regulations and directives.

Linking the choice of legal instrument to the question of delegation, one might expect that the tendency to delegate authority to the Commission would be stronger for regulations than for directives. The choice of the more 'supranational' regulations would signify a greater willingness to delegate power to the European level, while the inclination to use the more nationally sensitive directive would instead correspond to a greater hesitation to delegate. Moreover, and following the same logic, it is likely that policy areas, such as areas which are characterized by dynamic economic and technical developments, we would find a greater use of regulations than directives and a higher inclination to delegate to the Commission. The key issue is a concern with complexity and the need for specialized technical knowledge that gives legislators incentives to delegate. That such considerations play an important role is supported by empirical studies where such complexity is found to be the dominating explanation for variation in delegation to the Commission (Thomson and Torenvlied 2011).

CHALLENGES OF AGGREGATE DATA

Given the different nature of regulations and directives (even if that difference has faded over time) as well as the pronounced differences in the frequency of their use, on the whole as well as across policy areas, we emphasize that the differences characterizing these instruments should be borne in mind in order to understand the importance of the changing rules governing delegation. Studies of the causes of delegation, such as Franchino's study of the 'most important' EU laws, do not distinguish between the instruments but pools them and thereby possibly obscures differences related to the instruments as well as to the relevant policy areas.

However, the problem is more acute when we are dealing with aggregate numbers that do not distinguish between the importances of acts. According to Golub, failure to disaggregate directives from regulations entails conflating 'the most important areas of legislative decision making with administrative and routinized activity' (Golub 1999: 737). Distinguishing between legislated and Delegated Acts in this study, we are able to address the part of the problem that relates to administrative activity. The other part that Golub points to concerns the practice of adopting regulations in 'bulk packages', particularly in certain policy areas (von Bogdandy et al. 2004). Methodologically, this type of bias can be tackled in quantitative studies by a combination of sensitivity to policy area and controlling for quantitative differences between the number of measures adopted and those in force at any particular moment in time, as will be done in section 5.3.

Sensitivity to policy area is not just important for the methodological reasons described above. Rather, the characteristics of the policy area may leave their own mark. As Epstein and O'Halloran argue, the policy area is a strong determinant of the propensity to delegate in itself (Epstein and O'Halloran 1999). Differences in the level of complexity, technical knowledge, and/or the distributional consequences of different policy areas are likely to affect the delegation rate by influencing the costs and benefits of decision making by politicians (see Chapter 2). It is therefore important to take this into account when analysing delegation across policy areas.

Moreover, even a cursory look at production patterns in European law alerts the observer to pronounced differences in legislative activity in different policy areas. Failure to separate them in a causal analysis therefore runs the risk that trends in areas marked by high legislative activity may completely crowd out trends in less active areas. The dominant trends observed might in fact result from causal dynamics belonging to a specific legislative area. In Franchino's study of delegation in the EU, the analysis linking causes to effects is done on the sample of 158 measures as a whole (Franchino 2007). As Franchino himself shows, his sample (selected on the basis of citations in books about European law) contains a very uneven number of acts from different policy areas. The results of the statistical analysis may therefore underestimate effects in some fields, while overestimating them in others. Likewise, as suggested above, failure to distinguish between directives and regulations may also bias the results. Interestingly, the policy area most strongly represented in Franchino's sample is 'movement of persons'. In fact, this field constitutes 23 per cent of the total number of acts selected. However, out of the total number of legislated acts in the period investigated, the acts citing the relevant Treaty articles on which these are based (48–51/39–42) barely constitute 1 per cent of the total number of acts passed. Franchino himself comments on the 'imbalance' of representativity in quantitative terms that his selection method entails. It may be that the dynamics identified by Franchino in the sample characterize legislative action in the most important fields of legislation (i.e. the population he wants to describe); nonetheless, there is a high risk that the causalities and coefficients identified are characteristic of only a few policy areas and instruments rather than of all important legislation as such. In other words, one might suspect that the method used to identify important legislation (citations in books on EU-law; see Franchino 2007: ch. 3) implies a bias in favour of certain legislative areas at the expense of others.

However, taking policy fields into account in a major quantitative study, which refers not to a sample but to the entire population of legislated and delegated EU regulations and directives from 1970 to 2006, is methodologically challenging. Other quantitative studies of EU law have either failed to differentiate between policy fields or, on the basis of small samples, have used the Treaty legal base to distinguish between areas. As discussed in Appendix 1, this approach—due to our focus on Delegated Acts—is not viable in our case. A comprehensive description of the structure and trends in EU law (legislative and Delegated Acts), as undertaken here, is new. The detailed description of the method used can be found in Appendix 1.

5.2 Patterns and trends in legislative activity

5.2.1 *Patterns in legislative output of the European Community in the period 1970–2008*

The analysis of legislative activity is organized around four characteristics: the type of legal instrument; the time of adoption; the method of adoption; and the relevant policy area. The first two criteria are simple descriptors of legal acts. However, as regards the time dimension, we have chosen to present per annum data on the measures adopted each year, and we have included the number of measures in force at one particular moment in time. Both give important information about the pattern and structure of EU law, as we will discuss in section 5.3.3. With respect to policy area, there are various possibilities. As described in detail in Appendix 1, we use the directory codes to identify the policy content of the acts since they offer the most consistent indication of substantive content. Only eleven of the twenty possible directory codes—and thus policy areas—are included for the simple reason that only these contain a sufficient number of acts to make a quantitative presentation of patterns and trends meaningful (see Appendix 2).

Since directory codes may contain acts of different substantive content, we analysed the contents of these and found as follows. The legislated acts in the categories for Customs Union and Free Movement of Goods (CU), Agriculture (AG), Fisheries (FISH), Transport (TRANS), and Taxation (TAX) display a great degree of uniformity in terms of the Treaty articles on which they are based. A high (albeit) lesser degree of similarity in legal base is also observed for acts in External Relations (EXTER), Industrial Policy and Internal Market (IPIM), and Environment, Consumer & Health protection (ECH). Falling within a 'medium to high' range of similarity in legal base are acts pertaining to the Rights of Establishment and Freedom to Provide Services (REFS), Social Policy (SOC), and Competition (COMP).[8] About 15–25 per cent of the acts in any directory code are also classified in others, although acts classified in Taxation are not classified elsewhere. To a lesser extent, this is also true for Fisheries. Only the categories of Competition, External Relations, and Environment, Consumer, and Health Protection overlap with other categories at a rate of around 40 per cent. Finally, with respect to the method of adoption, i.e. delegation or non-delegation, the acts can be distinguished by author institution and by legal base. The presentation below classifies *Delegated* Acts as those adopted by the Commission,

---

[8] The acronyms for the policy areas (CU, AG, etc.) are our own and made for the purpose of data presentation. They are not used in the EUR-Lex database.

while acts adopted by the Council and the Parliament together or the Council alone are classified as *legislated* acts. This is a simple definition, which follows the logic of delegation presented in the theoretical chapter.

However, it should be observed that it is possible to employ other definitions that follow a different and to some extent more legal logic. Legal acts can thus be defined as legislated or delegated by reference to their legal basis rather than by adopting institution. Legislation citing a treaty article as legal base is commonly defined as legislated acts, as opposed to Delegated Acts, which refer to other legislation as its legal base. The Council can 'self-delegate' to its own bureaucratic institutions which adopt acts on the basis of legislation other than treaty articles. Likewise, the Commission may adopt laws that are directly based in a treaty article rather than other legislation. In presenting overall aggregate trends, the distinction is not very important. However, it plays a role in certain policy areas and it will therefore be discussed further in that context. The following descriptive analysis discusses the choice of instrument and method of adoption (delegation or legislation) across policy areas and over time.

THE AGGREGATE VIEW OF EU LEGISLATION: LEGISLATED AND DELEGATED DIRECTIVES AND REGULATIONS

As seen from Tables 5.1 and 5.2, regulations are by far the most preferred legislative instrument of the Commission and Council. Regulations constitute 92 per cent of the generally binding acts passed in the period under consideration and about 80 per cent of the legislation in force in 2008. However, the apparent imbalance in the choice of legal instrument is less pronounced in the group of legislated legal acts. Here regulations constitute slightly less than 80 per cent of the acts passed and only 56 per cent of the acts in force in 2008. In the group of Delegated Acts, the dominance of regulations is even stronger, with 94

Table 5.1 Regulations and directives passed 1970–2006

	Overview of European laws enacted 1970–2006					
	Legislated		Delegated		All	
Regulations	*6787* *79.5%*	*19.6%*	*27800* *96%*	*80.4%*	*34587* *92%*	*100%*
Directives	*1754* *20.5%*	*60%*	*1174* *4%*	*40%*	*2928* *8%*	*100%*
All	*8541* *100%*	*22.8%*	*28974* *100%*	*77.2%*	*37515* *100%*	*100%*

Table 5.2 Regulations and directives in force 2008 (September)

	Overview of European laws in force 2008					
	Legislated		Delegated		All	
Regulations	*1380*	*18.3%*	*6179*	*81.7%*	*7559*	*100%*
	56.3%		*79.9%*		*79.9%*	
Directives	*1070*	*56.4%*	*827*	*43.6%*	*1897*	*100%*
	43.7%		*11.8%*		*20.1%*	
All	*2450*	*25.9%*	*7006*	*74.1%*	*9456*	*100%*
	100%		*100%*		*100%*	

per cent of all the acts passed and 82 per cent of those in force. Hence, regulations are used much more frequently than directives in the legislative process. But the use of instruments is much more balanced when we take a snapshot of EU law in 2008. In other words, both legislated and delegated regulations are more frequently amended and/or encompass acts of shorter duration than is the case for directives.

Furthermore, the balance between the number of legislated and Delegated Acts is clearly different for each type of instrument. The balance of legislated and Delegated Acts for both instruments is 20/80 for regulations and 40/60 for directives, irrespective of whether we look at the legislation adopted over time or in force. This pattern lends credibility to the expected existence of a common motive—namely, retention of power at the level of the nation state—behind both the choice of legal instrument and the decision to delegate legislative powers (see Chapters 4–6). Moreover, the lack of difference—in proportional terms—between the legislated and Delegated Acts adopted and in force for both instruments indicates the same share of amendments and/or short-lived acts for Delegated Acts and legislated acts of both types. In absolute numbers, however, the difference between acts passed and those in force is largest for the group of delegated regulations followed by legislated regulations, legislated directives, and delegated directives. In other words, at the aggregate level the delegated directive appears to be the most durable and/or subject to fewer amendments and the delegated regulation the least durable and/or most amended type of instrument. However, the delegated directive is also the most infrequent type, constituting just 3 per cent of all acts adopted and 9 per cent of those in force. On the whole, delegated directives are the least frequent type of act found, while the most frequent type is the delegated regulation (see also Appendix 4).

It should be noted that the pattern identified for legislation in force differs somewhat from the one found by von Bogdandy et al. based on a sample of 500 EU laws (von Bogdandy et al. 2004). In their sample, a group of legislated acts, the balance between regulations and directives is practically the same, and the share of directives is somewhat smaller in the group of Delegated Acts (6 per cent compared to 12 per cent). For regulations, however, they find a clearly higher share of legislated than Delegated Acts (31/69 instead of the 18/82). This is also the case for directives, although the difference here is much more pronounced, with 30 per cent more legislated directives in their sample than in the 2008 population (84/16 instead of 56/44). These differences could be explained by the time difference (2008 versus 1997) and by the fact that they study a sample rather than the population of EU legislative acts. However, a more likely explanation of the sizable differences is that they stem from the data source. Von Bogdandy et al. rely on the Directory of Community Legislation in force which, as they say, does not 'include legal acts from the so-called "day-to-day" administration, especially the multitude of short-lived regulations from the agricultural sector' and also 'does not list amendments independently, but under the amended act' (von Bogdandy et al. 2004: 93).

EUR-Lex includes all such acts and therefore presents a different picture. It could be expected that the Delegated Acts include more short-lived and frequently amended acts than do the legislated ones and this may explain the difference in the findings. It also highlights the importance of distinguishing between policy areas, where the 'turnover' of legislation is expected to differ significantly. This pattern will be explored in the next section.

5.3 Policy area and legal instrument

Are there differences in the use of legal instruments across policy areas? From existing research (Epstein and O'Halloran 1999; Franchino 2007) we would expect to find differences in the choice of legal instrument as well as the propensity to delegate. The findings indicated in Tables 5.3 and 5.4 confirm this expectation. As mentioned in Section 5.2.1, the policy areas included are Customs Union and Free Movement of Goods (CU), Agriculture (AG), Fisheries (FISH), Social Policy (SOC), Right of Establishment and Freedom to Provide Services (REFS), Transport (TRANS), Competition (COMP), Taxation (TAX), External Relations (EXTER), Industrial Policy and Internal Market (IPIM) and Environment, Consumers, and Health Protection (ECH). A precise understanding of the type of legislation included in the different categories can be obtained by looking at the tables in Appendix 2. It is perhaps

Table 5.3 Regulations and directives enacted 1970–2006

	Regulations and Directives enacted 1970–2006											
DC:	CU	AG	FISH	SOC	REFS	TRANS	COMP	TAX	EXTER	IPIM	ECH	Total
Regulations Number	7731	19427	2942	164	34	278	107	28	6262	354	546	37873
Pct	20.4	51.3	7.8	0.4	0.1	0.7	0.3	0.1	16.5	0.9	1.5	100
Directives Number	62	963	2	110	201	231	25	129	9	1167	407	3306
Pct	1.9	29.1	0.1	3.3	6.1	7.0	0.8	3.9	0.2	35.3	12.3	100
Regulations of total	99%	95%	100%	60%	14%	55%	81%	18%	100%	23%	57%	92%

Table 5.4 Regulations and directives in force 2008

	Regulations and Directives in force 2008											
DC:	CU	AG	FISH	SOC	REFS	TRANS	COMP	TAX	EXTER	IPIM	ECH	Total
Regulations Number	910	4145	707	94	37	202	55	24	1075	193	461	7903
Pct	11.5%	52.4%	8.9%	1.2%	0.5%	2.6%	0.7%	0.4%	13.6%	2.4%	5.8%	100%
Directives Number	14	626	2	75	101	164	2	71	5	858	285	2203
Pct	0.6%	28.4%	0.1%	3.4%	4.6%	7.4%	0.2%	3.3%	0.2%	38.9%	12.9%	100%
Regulations of total	98%	87%	100%	56%	27%	55%	96%	25%	100%	18%	62%	78%

particularly important to note that the legislation in the category of EXTER for the major part covers legislation based in the common agricultural and commercial policies, and to a lesser extent legislation related to international agreements and development cooperation.

5.3.1 *Policy Area, Legal Instrument, and Legislative Activity*

For regulations the distribution of acts across areas is highly uneven. The vast majority of the total sum of regulations stems from one of four areas, namely CU, AG, FISH, and EXTER. In fact, 96 per cent of 'all' regulations passed in the thirty-six years of European cooperation and 86 per cent of those in force in 2008 fall into one of these four policy categories. Over 50 per cent fall into the category of AG alone whether we look at legislation in force or legislation adopted.[9]

Directives display a slightly more even distribution between areas, and the policy areas that account for most legislative activity are not the same as for regulations. The three categories of AG, IPIM, and finally ECH protection are the dominant ones. On their own they account for around 80 per cent of the total number of directives adopted in the period, and the same is true for directives in force in 2008. AG is the only policy area that is placed among the most legislatively active when both instruments are considered.

It is therefore clear that quantitative analyses that look at the aggregate developments in legislative activity will be strongly influenced by particular characteristics and trends within certain policy areas. AG, where over half the regulations and about one-third of all regulations have been classified, will tend to dominate the picture. This reveals the danger of quantitative studies that present the legislative output of the EC/EU in aggregate terms over time and purport to draw conclusions concerning the activity of the European institutions on the whole. If we look at directives only, as Golub did to explore whether there is 'eurosclerosis' (Golub 1999), there is an extremely high risk of committing an ecological fallacy. Changes in legislative activity in either the areas of IPIM or AG are likely to drown out contrary trends in all other areas of EU action simply because they constitute such a high share of the total. Although we do not consider time here, our later analyses will show that this conclusion holds.

The share of regulations as a proportion of the total number of acts adopted/in force is a good indicator of differences in the use of

---

[9] Some caution is required when relying on the exact proportions. The summary figure given here represents an overestimate due to the fact that, as noted earlier, many legal acts are classified in more than one directory code.

instruments across policy areas. As could be expected from the aggregate figures, the most common occurrence is that regulations make up the larger part. The four areas that account for 96 per cent of all regulations are also individually strongly biased towards regulations (87–100 per cent of total acts). Hence, in these highly active legislative areas, directives play a marginal role—at least in quantitative terms. This is also the case for Competition policy, which at the aggregate level accounts for a smaller share. The areas of SOC, TRANS, and ECH protection show a more balanced use of regulations and directives. A few policy areas stand out, however, because the number of directives exceeds the number of regulations. Thus, in the area of IPIM, where 35 per cent of all directives are classified, only 20 per cent of the legal acts adopted and in force are regulations. For the REFS and TAX, the dominance of directives is even more pronounced.

This finding raises the question of what might explain these differences in the choice of instrument. As mentioned above, there are two possible considerations that may come into play when deciding on an instrument. One is the 'objective' desirability of the uniformity of the legal regime; the other is the sensitivity to national legal systems or, put differently, the balance of power between the Community and the individual member states with respect to policymaking. These considerations come into play ex ante when deciding on a choice of instrument when designing the Treaties, or in the course of the day-to-day functioning of the EU institutions.

In general, one would expect a certain correspondence between the nature of the EU's competences across policy areas and the use of legal instrument. The legal literature—and, in some instances, the ECJ—divide the EU competences into three types: exclusive competence (applying to a part of Fisheries policy, the Monetary policy, and the Common commercial policy); shared competence (applying to most policies); and a subordinate type of competence consisting of measures that support, coordinate, or supplement actions of the member states (typical for Public health, Culture, Education, etc.). One would, therefore, expect that policy areas where the Community has exclusive competences would be governed by means of the more supranational instrument. And indeed, both Common commercial policy and Fisheries measures feature strongly. But this explanation does not account for all the observed variation. Another obvious explanation for variation in the use of instruments is the legal basis: to what extent does the legal basis, and thereby the outcome of Treaty negotiations, determine the variation?

Table 5.5 shows the percentage of legislated acts that cite a Treaty article which calls for the use of a directive, and the percentage of

Table 5.5 Regulations/directives ratio and Treaty dictated use of legal instrument

		TREATY DICTATED USE OF INSTRUMENT										
		CU	AG	FISH	SOC	REFS	TRANS	COMP	TAX	EXTER	IP&IM	ECH
Regulation	*enacted*	99%	95%	100%	60%	14%	55%	81%	18%	100%	23%	57%
Share of total	*in force*	98%	87%	100%	56%	27%	55%	96%	25%	100%	18%	62%
Treaty decision	Share of acts enacted	0%	1%	0%	12%	70%	4%	10%	53%	0%	33%	22%
of Directives	citing either of these											
Treaty Article Number												
TEEC (Original; SEA) TEC (Maastricht			100	103	100	54, 57, 66, 100	100	90	100		100	100
TEC (Amsterdam; Nice)					137	47, 55, 95		86	93, 94, 96		47, 55	95

regulations of the total (both legislated and delegated) in each policy area. The figures clearly show that there is a close connection. In the articles relevant for the policy areas scrutinized here, the Treaties only mention a required instrument for directives. The incidence of legislated legal acts that cite a Treaty article requiring the use of directives is either absent or extremely low in the directory codes that have very high shares of regulations. Conversely, the policy areas where directives are the dominant instrument are also the areas where the legal bases most frequently cited require the use of directives. A simple correlation of the share of regulations as a proportion of the total number of acts adopted with the share of legislated acts citing the latter gives a very high negative Pearson's R of −0.90.[10] This correlation is extremely high, but this does not indicate a determined relationship between Treaty base and instrument in the sense that directives are only used when it is required by the legal base.

As can be seen from the percentages given, there is a higher use of directives than that which is directly required by the treaties. For instance, for Industrial Policy and Internal Market, 33 per cent of the legislated acts cite a Treaty article that requires the use of directives, but 77 per cent of the legislated acts adopted and 82 per cent of those in force in 2008 are directives. What it does mean, however, is that the free choice exercised by the European bodies when selecting instruments in the daily functioning of the EU closely mirrors the choices made at the Treaty level for each policy area. A major part of the explanation may be that there has been a tendency for parallelism of instruments between the basic act and the implementing acts. The ECJ has clarified that there is no such principle, but in practice it appears to have had an influence on instrument choice for Delegated Acts (von Bogdandy et al. 2004: 100).

5.3.2 *The use of delegation in different policy areas*

LEGISLATED AND DELEGATED REGULATIONS

As observed earlier, the share of delegated regulations as a proportion of the total number of regulations, i.e. 73–82 per cent, is very high for acts adopted and acts in force. Moving down from the aggregate level and observing delegation shares in different policy areas reveals a highly differentiated pattern—and more so than what was observed for the choice of instrument. Delegated Acts constitute only 34 per cent of the

---

[10] Significant at the 0.01 level.

Table 5.6 Regulations adopted

		REGULATIONS (enacted 1970–2006)										
		CU	AG	FISH	SOC	REFS	TRANS	COMP	TAX	EXTER	IPIM	ECH	Total
Legislated	pct.	2856	3373	990	115	14	165	36	10	2434	113	146	10252
		27.9%	32.9%	9.7%	1.1%	0.1%	1.6%	0.4%	0.1%	23.7%	1.1%	1.4%	100%
Delegated	pct.	4902	16077	1960	57	19	115	72	18	3832	242	405	27699
		17.7%	58.0%	7.1%	0.2%	0.1%	0.4%	0.2%	0.1%	13.8%	0.9%	1.5%	100%
Share Delegated		63%	83%	66%	33%	58%	41%	67%	64%	61%	68%	74%	73%

Table 5.7 Regulations in force

		REGULATIONS (in force 2008)										
		CU	AG	FISH	SOC	REFS	TRANS	COMP	TAX	EXTER	IPIM	ECH	Total
Legislated	number pct.	210	298	151	51	15	102	28	6	441	61	70	1433
		14.6%	20.8%	10.5%	3.6%	1.1%	7.1%	2.0%	0.4%	30.7%	4.3%	4.9%	100%
Delegated	pct.	700	3847	556	43	22	100	27	18	634	132	132	6211
		10.8%	59.5%	8.6%	0.7%	0.4%	1.5%	0.4%	0.3%	9.8%	2.0%	6.0%	100%
Share Delegated		77%	93%	79%	46%	59%	50	49%	75%	59	68%	85%	82%

total number of acts adopted in some areas and over 90 per cent in others. At the high end, AG stands out, with over 90 per cent of the acts regulating this area by means of the comitology system; but other areas such as FISH, ECH, CU, and TAX are not far behind. Only two areas, namely SOC and TRANS, distinguish themselves by having more—or the same—number of legislated as compared to Delegated Acts adopted or in force. This is also the case for COMP when we look at the delegation shares of legislation in force, while the share for legislation adopted is much higher.

As might be expected from the aggregate numbers presented in Tables 5.8 and 5.9 below, the generally dominant pattern is reversed when we look at directives. Only a few areas, including CU, AG, and FISH, have the same or higher number of delegated directives as legislated ones. In all other policy areas, the exact opposite is the case. External affairs has a zero share of delegated directives, but directives are also rarely used in this area (about 1 to 700 regulations). In the areas of SOC and TAX, as described above, directives are frequently used, but the share of Delegated Acts is extremely low. Moreover, it is notable that the delegation shares are—without exception, in all policy areas—much lower than the share of regulations, whether we look at acts adopted over time or a snapshot of those in force (see also Appendix 3).

If we distinguish Delegated Acts from legislated acts by legal basis (secondary legislation versus Treaty article) instead of adopting institution, this does not change the overall pattern observed. However, it does modify it somewhat. Of the acts adopted by the Council—categorized as legislated acts above—a significant portion are based in other legislation (not Treaty articles). In the areas of AG, 43 per cent, FISH, 60 per cent, and EXTER, 35 per cent of the legal acts are instances of 'self-delegation', while the proportion of such laws in other areas is negligible—i.e. around 5 per cent or less. All three areas are examples of high delegation areas and therefore changing definition from adopting institution to legal basis does not change the substantive conclusions. Of the acts adopted by the Commission, only in the area of Competition is there a significant share of laws citing a Treaty article rather than other legislation as its legal basis (25 per cent) (see tables in Appendix 5). Classifying such acts as instances of legislation in the sense of legal acts authored by the principals in the EU would, however, not make sense in the context of the theoretical framework. In legal terms, this is an important distinction.

As pointed out, we may expect a correspondence between the propensity to use directives as the main legal instrument in a given area and the disinclination to use delegation. The reason for this is that the motive

Table 5.8 Directives enacted 1970–2006

	CU	AG	FISH	SOC	REFS	TRANS	COMP	TAX	EXTER	IPIM	ECH	Total
						DIRECTIVES (enacted 1970–2006)						
Legislated	30	469	2	108	172	172	12	125	9	665	301	2065
pct.	1.5%	22.7%	0.1%	5.2%	8.3%	8.3%	0.6%	6.1%	0.4%	32.2%	14.6%	100.0%
Delegated	33	448	1	10	23	58	13	4	0	505	106	1201
pct.	2.8%	37%	0.2%	1.1%	1.9%	5%	1.2%	0%	0.0%	42%	8.8%	100.0%
Share Delegated	52%	49%	33%	8%	12%	25%	52%	3%	0%	43%	26%	37%

Table 5.9 Directives in force 2008

	CU	AG	FISH	SOC	REFS	TRANS	COMP	TAX	EXTER	IPIM	ECH	Total
						DIRECTIVES (in force 2008)						
Legislated	12	222	1	71	89	116	0	67	5	432	205	1220
pct.	1.0%	18.2%	0.1%	5.8%	7.3%	9.5%	0.0%	5.5%	0.4%	35.4%	16.8%	100.0%
Delegated	2	404	1	4	12	48	2	4	0	426	80	983
pct.	0.2%	41.2%	0.1%	0.4%	1.2%	4.9%	0.1%	0.3%	0.0%	43.4%	8.2%	100.0%
Share Delegated	14%	65%	50%	5%	12%	29%	100%	6%	0%	50%	28%	45%

Table 5.10 Relationship between instrument and delegation rates

		DOMINANCE OF REGULATIONS		
DELEGATION		High	Medium	Low
	High	Agriculture Fisheries External Relations Customs Union		
	Medium	Competition	Environment, Consumers, and Health	Industrial Policy and Inner Market
	Low		Social Policy Transport	Right of Establishment Taxation

for using a certain legal instrument may not just be to establish a 'technical' degree of uniformity of legal language, but is rather to maintain latitude for national authorities. We would therefore expect delegation rates to be lower for directives than for regulations. This is clearly the case. But we also find that policy areas characterized by a more pronounced use of directives than regulations are also areas with significantly lower delegation rates for both directives and regulations.

Table 5.10 plots the relationship between the dominance of regulations as legal instruments and the propensity to use delegation as the method for adopting acts in a specific policy area. The dominance of regulations is simply measured by the percentage of all acts (directives and regulations) that are regulations. The frequency of Delegated Acts is a combined measure reflecting the share of delegation in regulations and directives weighted by their respective shares of the total number of legal acts.[11] As can be seen from the table, the pattern is clearly one of strong association between the variables. For instance, all five areas but one (Competition policy) where regulations stand out as the preferred legal instrument also have a high delegation rate. Although some small deviations from a clearly linear pattern can be observed, it emerges that none of the policy areas falls completely outside the pattern. There are no cases in the extreme corners of low delegation/high share of regulation and high delegation/low share of regulations.

Expressed more systematically, the association between the share of regulations and the rate of delegation, measured by the correlation

[11] That is to say, the share of delegated directives is weighted by the share of directives as a proportion of the total number of acts and added to a similarly weighted measure for regulations: Delegation share = (Delegated Directives + Delegated Regulations)/All Directives & Regulations.

Table 5.11 Legislation enacted

CORRELATION		
Pearson's R	*Regulation share*	
	Per 5 yrs	*Annual*
Delegation Directives	0.48**	0.43**
Delegation Regulations	0.43**	0.58**
Delegation Combined	0.74**	0.67**

** *significant at the 0.01 level.*

Table 5.12 Legislation in force

CORRELATION	
Pearson's R	*Regulation Share*
	Annual
Delegation Directives	0.27**
Delegation Regulations	0.75**
Delegation combined	0.73**

** *significant at the 0.01 level.*

coefficient Pearson's R, is strong. In Table 5.11 correlation is shown between the two variables at two levels of aggregation, i.e. per 1-year and 5-year periods. The 5-year period was included for two reasons. First, there are many missing values for directives when the shares are calculated on an annual basis; and second, the legislative pattern is likely to be more subject to random fluctuations when we look at individual years. And as the table shows, the Pearson's R between the variables is also highest when the 5-year period serves as the unit of analysis. It is the very high Pearson's R of 0.74 that indicates that the overall frequency of delegated legislation in different policy areas is extremely closely associated with a predominant use of regulations.

It was to be expected from the aggregate data that areas with a dominance of regulations would also reveal the use of many delegated regulations, since regulations are the most frequent type of legal act. However, it was not a foregone conclusion that variation in the dominance of regulations across policy areas would also be associated with a higher share of delegated, as opposed to legislated, directives. This association is, however, strongly supported by the data and shows very little sensitivity to the level of aggregation of the data with respect to time. The analysis thus provides evidence of a strong connection between the use of the most supranational legal instrument and use of the delegated legislation across policy areas. We may therefore conclude that a common underlying logic of intergovernmentalism versus supranationalism is at work in the legislative process, which manifests itself similarly with respect to choice of instrument and of decision-making body.

Finally, one may speculate about what might cause these differences across policy areas. From the data presented, the policy areas of CU, AG, FISH, COMP, and EXTER—according to their choice of instruments— could be characterized as policy fields where—compared to other areas—there is a particular functional need to have uniform regulatory regimes. Judging by the proportion of delegation, we could surmise that in these areas there is a higher need for expertise, a higher degree of uncertainty—substantive or political—and a stronger need to establish credible commitments or blame-shifting than in other areas of policy-making. To answer these questions, careful studies of the policy areas would be required; such endeavours are outside the scope of this book.

5.3.3 *Temporal developments in European law*

We finally raise an important question concerning developments over time: Is there a tendency for increased use of one of the instruments? Does delegation become more frequent when adopting legal acts? Do policy areas converge in the use of instruments and the propensity to delegate, or do differences persist between policy areas?

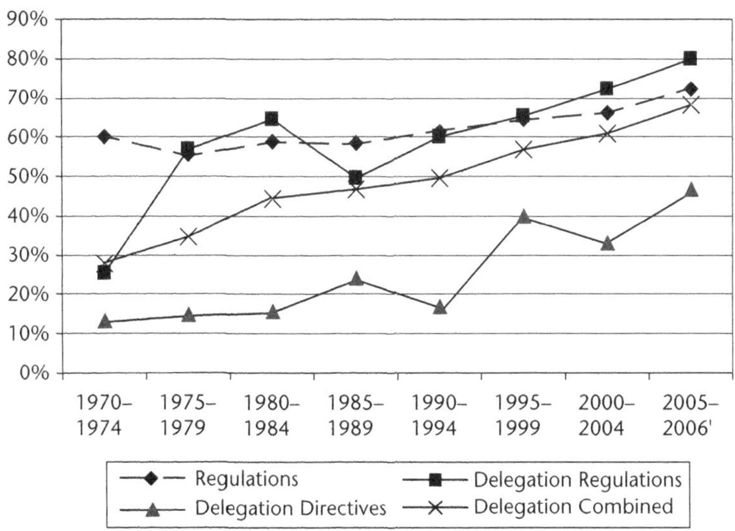

Figure 5.1 Legislative Patterns over Time

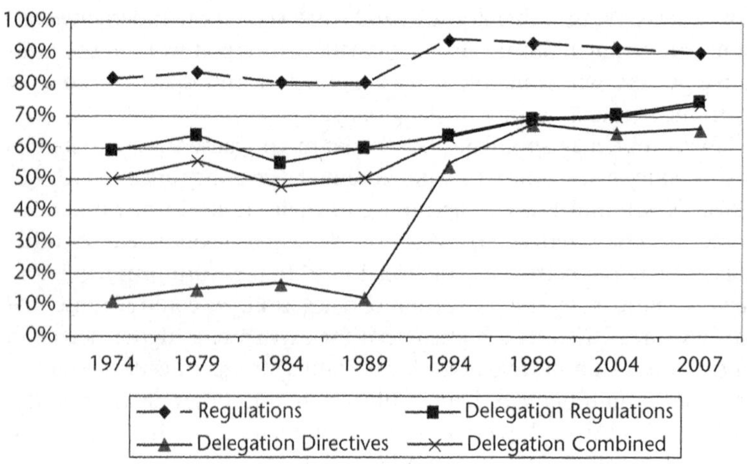

Figure 5.2 Structure of EU Law over Time

Figure 5.1 shows the aggregate developments over time for the policy areas under investigation. The pattern clearly shows a moderate and steady increase in the number of regulations passed per year since the late 1980s, but with no apparent trend in the decades before. An even more consistent upward trend can be observed for the passage of delegated law. The combined development of delegation regulations and directives displays a consistently strong upward trend from the beginning to the end of the examined period. At the beginning of the 1970s, delegated legislation constituted about one quarter of the legislative output, but as of the early 1990s Delegated Acts exceed the number of legislated acts. At present, there are some two Delegated Acts for each legislated act. For directives alone the increased share of delegation is from 13 to 47 per cent, while regulations have remained at a higher level throughout, rising from 26 to 80 per cent. Some increase in the share of Delegated Acts over time might be expected, as each legislative act that is passed potentially provides a basis for Delegated Acts (the 'natural growth' phenomenon). We might therefore expect an upward trend both in terms of acts adopted and in terms of the acts in force each year. In any case, the data show a clear and very strong upward tendency. This finding raises the question of whether the observed increase in the use of regulations and delegated legislation is a universal tendency, or whether it is limited to some policy fields.

As regards the balance between regulations and directives, the aggregate tendency towards regulations as the preferred instrument is not

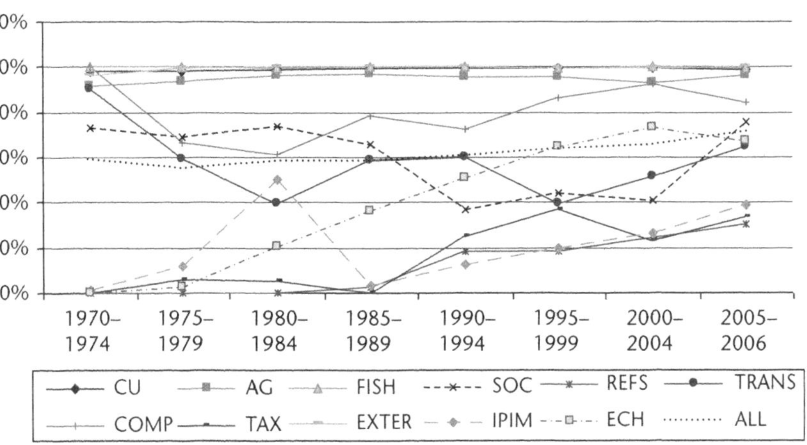

Figure 5.3 Share of Regulation in Each Policy Area

evident in all policy areas. For the four areas of CU, AG, FISH, and EXTER, the level has been very high throughout the period—equal to or close to 100 per cent—obviously leaving no space for further increase in the share of regulations. An unambiguous upward trend can, however, be observed in the policy areas of REFS, TAX, and ECH. Similarly, there is an increase in the share of regulations for IPIM, although the pattern of gradual increase is broken by a very high share of regulations in the mid-1980s, which in later years is not repeated. In other words, the baseline of comparison matters. If the mid-1980s were the starting point, regulations would appear to have decreased rather than increased their share. The question is what is reflected by the observed trend towards increased dominance of regulation in these four areas.

For the area of REFS for instance, it is possible that the change towards using regulation instead of directives for the approximation of laws provides part of the explanation. The proportion of laws in this section that cite Treaty articles from the area of TRANS, which is heavily dominated by regulations, is another possible contributing factor. In the area of TAX, the number of laws is limited, but here changes in instrument used for the approximation of laws may play a part; but since it only constitutes a small part, it is more likely that regulations have increasingly become the preferred instrument to deal with harmonization of indirect taxation that is the aim of most laws in the area. It is plausible, however, that the trend in the categories of IPIM is attributable to changes in use of the law for the approximation of laws, since this is an important legal base for legislation in this category.

The same consideration might contribute to explaining the consistent increase since the mid-1970s in the proportion of regulations in the areas of ECH. An investigation into the micro-foundations of the trends observed here would, however, be an independent research question and is beyond the scope of this study. As mentioned earlier, there are numerous pitfalls when interpreting aggregate trends in legislation and caution must therefore be observed.

Finally, in the areas of SOC, COMP, and TRANS, no clear trend is observable; the levels both rise and fall quite substantially during the period of observation. It should also be noted that in these three areas the total number of legal acts is low and therefore a few regulations or directives adopted may cause big shifts in the shares observed.

In terms of the proportion of delegation out of the total legislative output, the trend is more universal across policy areas, although some differences stand out. For the areas of AG and FISH, the share of delegated legislation was very high from the outset (over 80 per cent). Only an overall steady increase can be observed for AG. The other policy areas start at lower shares, but all, without exception, experience an increase from the beginning to the end of the period, even if the development has not been one of steady increase but in some cases rather one of fluctuation.

Finally, as already observed, there are significant differences between the policy areas in terms of legislative output. However, it is also interesting to see the trends over time in legislative activity. Figure 5.5 shows the number of acts adopted in each area relative to the number adopted

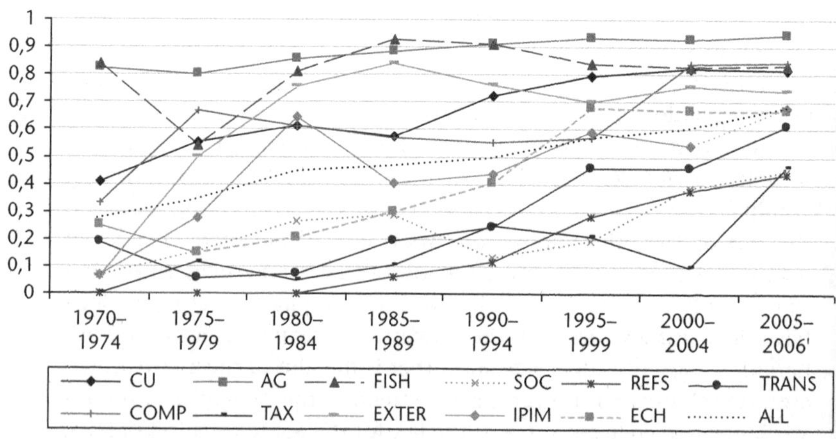

Figure 5.4 Combined Delegation Share

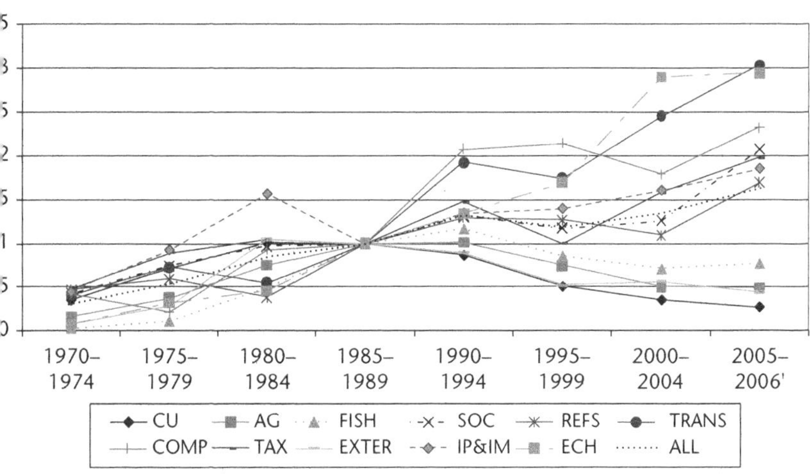

Figure 5.5 Relative Legislative Activity of Policy Areas

in the period 1985–9. The areas of CU, AG, FISH, and EXTER, which are similar in the sense of having had consistently high shares of regulation and delegated legislation, also follow a remarkably similar pattern of increased activity until the late 1980s or early 1990s, since when there has been a decline. In most cases (except CU) the number of acts adopted per year is higher now than it was in the early 1970s, but the differences are relatively small. For all other areas there is a clear increase over the relevant time period. The largest increases relative to early levels are clearly seen for TRANS and ECH. These are followed by COMP, SOC, TAX, and REFS.

5.4 Conclusion

This analysis of legislative output of the European Union has documented the overall structure and developmental trends with respect to the type of legislation (instrument) and the procedures for its adoption (legislation/delegation) overall and in different policy areas. The results show that there is great variation not only in legislative activity, but also in the use of regulations and directives, as well as delegation in the adoption of laws across policy areas. At the aggregate level, regulations have become increasingly dominant over time. However, the analysis by

Table 5.13 Overview of instrument and delegation share per policy area

		Regulations share			Combined Delegation share		
		Pct.	St.Dev.	Trend	All years	St.Dev.	Trend
Customs Union and Free Movement of Goods	enacted	99%	1%	*Stable*	64%	17%	moderate increase
	in force	98%	2%	*Stable*	62%	20%	moderate increase
Agriculture	enacted	95%	3%	*Stable*	89%	6%	moderate increase
	in force	92%	2%	*Stable*	69%	11%	very high increase
Fisheries	enacted	100%	0%	*Stable*	86%	16%	moderate increase
	in force	97%	1%	*Stable*	49%	13%	very high increase
Social Policy	enacted	60%	27%	*Fluctuating*	24%	22%	very high increase
	in force	68%	14%	*Fluctuating*	13%	10%	very high increase
Right of Establishment and Freedom to Provide Services	enacted	14%	16%	*Increase*	16%	20%	very high increase
	in force	20%	27%	*Very high increase*	15%	20%	very high increase
Transport	enacted	55%	23%	*Fluctuating*	34%	24%	very high increase
	in force	71%	11%	*Decrease*	22%	11%	very high increase
Competition	enacted	81%	29%	*Fluctuating*	65%	42%	moderate increase
	in force	95%	5%	*Stable*	54%	9%	moderate increase
Taxation	enacted	18%	23%	*Increase*	17%	22%	very high increase
	in force	20%	23%	*Very high increase*	17%	20%	very high increase
External Relations	enacted	100%	5%	*Stable*	74%	28%	high increase
	in force	98%	3%	*Stable*	26%	9%	very high increase
Industrial Policy and Inner Market	enacted	23%	18%	*Increase*	49%	23%	high increase
	in force	20%	22%	*Very high increase*	17%	20%	very high increase
Environment, Consumers, and Health Protection	enacted	57%	29%	*Increase*	55%	26%	high increase
	in force	31%	32%	*Very high increase*	33%	26%	very high increase

directory codes showed that this trend towards a higher use of regulations can in fact only be observed in three policy areas. The other areas evince either stable shares of regulations and directives, or fluctuations with no identifiable tendency towards increase or decrease. With respect to the number of acts adopted under delegation, the aggregate trend towards a higher share of Delegated Acts is also observable in each policy area. Here the differentiation lies mainly in the degree of change in the period under observation.

The expected connection between legal instrument and the use of delegation also found ample support in the data. The correlation between variables measuring the share of regulations and of delegation was consistently high *regardless* of the level of aggregation and whether it was measured on delegation for directives, regulations, or a combined value. This lends support to the argument that the same factors that influence the likelihood of delegation also influence the choice of legal instrument. Regulation is the more supranational instrument of the two in the sense that it generally deprives the member states of the right to legislate in an area, while directives typically leave more scope for national action. In the policy areas that rely most heavily on directives, a low number of Delegated Acts is also typically adopted.

The pronounced differences between policy areas in terms of legislative activity, choice of instrument, and delegation rates confirm that quantitative studies of delegation should be wary of drawing conclusions on the basis of data where there has been no differentiation on the basis of legal instruments on the one hand, and policy area on the other. The characteristics appear so clearly differentiated that sensitivity to both instrument and policy area is required to understand the logic of delegation and to shed light on the facts that influence it.

In the next quantitative empirical chapters we investigate how a specific change of institutional rule impacts upon the willingness of the Commission, the Council, and the Parliament to engage in delegated legislation. Referring to the findings of this chapter, where it was pointed out that delegation as compared to legislation has clearly increased, starting in the early 1990s (p. 118) when co-decision was introduced, we first focus on the question of how co-decision impacted on the preferences for delegation of the Commission, the Council, and the Parliament. In a further chapter, we analyse the impact of the revised comitology decision on the respective preferences of the Commission and the Council.

6

The impact of co-decision on comitology: Environmental policy

In Chapters 6 and 7, we focus on the Council, the Commission, and the European Parliament's preferences for either legislation or delegation and, if the latter is chosen, for the specific comitology procedure to be used. Given a specific institutional rule, we analyse the Commission's propensity to propose delegation and the willingness of the legislator(s) to adopt these proposals. We also examine whether these preferences shift when the rules change. As we know, the co-decision procedure substantially increased the Parliament's role in legislation, but left its competences in the comitology committees untouched. Hence, alterations in the legislative rule from cooperation/consultation to co-decision are likely to affect all institutional actors and their willingness both to delegate and to favour a particular type of comitology committee.

6.1 Hypotheses

Two explanations may be offered for the choice of legislation or delegation to comitology and, in the case of the latter, for the choice of a specific comitology procedure. As developed in the theoretical chapter, one explanation is based on principal–agent theory which emphasizes how delegation often occurs in order to save transaction costs. Another explanation constituting the core of our argument in this book is based on distributive bargaining theory in a given institutional context. Both explanations share similar assumptions of bounded rationality, transaction costs, and incomplete contracts, and predict similar results. However, the underlying causal mechanisms leading to the outcomes are different.

The first argument proposes an increase in efficiency by choosing delegation over legislation: delegation saves transaction costs of bargaining over the details of legislation, the collection of detailed information, and having to engage in high side-payments to accommodate diverse interests and build a majority or consensus. Scholars using this transaction cost-saving argument for delegation also submit that delegation is more likely when principals are divided over issues, but that these principals therefore also have a strong incentive to control the agent. Following this argument, it could be defended that the introduction of co-decision, which obliges the Council to negotiate with the EP as an equal partner in legislation, increases the transaction costs of reaching agreement and hence will lead to increased delegation with extensive control.

Second, the increasing use of delegation and comitology rules favouring specific institutional actors may also be interpreted as a contest for power between institutional actors who seek to maximize their influence over institutional competences and thereby their influence over policy outcomes. We argue that, *under given institutional rules*, actors' preferences for delegation will be a function of whether the actor has more ability to influence policy through delegation or through legislation, and that those preferences change as the attractiveness of pursuing legislation (or the lack of it) changes. In other words, actors' preferences for delegation will be determined by the degree to which they have effective influence over policy that is carried out through delegation as opposed to legislation. As a result, they will press for the widespread use of procedures that favour their own interests and for less frequent use (and, where possible, the alteration or abandonment) of those procedures that do not.

The introduction of co-decision involved a relative loss of legislative power for the Council; and the necessity for the Commission to take into account a second legislator that may or may not support its proposal. In Chapter 2, we develop our expectations about the Commissions' meta-preferences and strategic preference and argue that the Commission would prefer delegation to co-decision.

H3 With increasing legislative competences of the Parliament under co-decision, the Commission will be more inclined to propose delegation to comitology.

With regard to the type of comitology procedure, we present the following rival hypotheses: The Commission—with an increasing number of delegation proposals—is either true to its meta-preferences and proposes the least constraining procedure; or the Commission strategically anticipates the Council's opposition[1] to the least constraining comitology procedures and proposes more restrictions for acts that could alternatively be adopted solely through legislation.[2]

> *H4a With an increasing number of delegation proposals, the Commission will propose the least constraining procedures, e.g. advisory and management committees.*
>
> *H4b With an increasing number of delegation proposals, the Commission will propose the more restrictive comitology procedure, e.g. regulatory committees.*

The Council, for its part, may seek to delegate more frequently to comitology after the empowerment of the EP in legislation. This would allow the Council to maximize the control it can exercise over decision making and to eschew the relative loss of decision-making power under co-decision. It may also motivate the Council to choose comitology committees that allow for the maximum influence of member state representatives.

> *H5 With increasing legislative competences of the Parliament under co-decision, the Council will be inclined to delegate more to comitology.*
>
> *H6 The increase in delegation accepted by the Council will be accompanied by an increase in the use of the regulatory committee.*

We expect that the increased willingness of the Commission and Council to delegate will start in the period following the signature of a treaty introducing co-decision and preceding its entrance into force, with the Commission and the Council anticipating the loss of power as a consequence of co-decision, but still being in a position to delegate without having to face a veto of the Parliament. While it is true that the Commission and Council might technically adopt detailed legislation on their own in this in-between period, they are also aware that such detailed legislation would probably need to be amended. Hence, both

---

[1] The Commission, obviously, also anticipates Parliament's preferences—especially when the co-decision procedure is used. However, those preferences are not clear. On the one hand, it has been shown that the Parliament's preferences are traditionally closer to those of the Commission (Napel and Widgrén 2008) and hence it might be expected that the Parliament would tend to favour the committees in which the Commission has more autonomy. On the other hand, in some specific policy fields—including the environment—the Parliament prefers the Commission to be controlled by a third party rather than acting alone (interview with Commission officials, March 2005 and April 2006).

[2] Legal reasons could also be behind the probable objection of the Council to the advisory and management committees—as the Council's Comitology Decision states that regulatory committees should be used in the case of 'measures of general scope designed to apply essential provisions of basic instruments' and to the updating or adaptation of 'certain non-essential provisions of the instrument', i.e. in the case of measures which could alternatively be passed by legislation.

actors will have incentives to delegate as much as possible before the imminent coming into effect of co-decision.

Finally, we expect that—with the introduction of co-decision—the Parliament will insist on legislation and oppose delegation:

H7 With the introduction of co-decision, the Parliament will seek to veto delegation and press for legislation only.

6.2 Databases

Our database uses the EU's EUR-Lex and PreLex online catalogues, which include the full text of all Commission proposals and parliamentary amendments that have been made since 1994, thus enabling us to investigate proposals over a period of fourteen years (up to June 2006). EUR-Lex (formerly Celex) enables us to select all Commission proposals in full text based on a given treaty article and to identify the resulting final legislation as adopted by the Council (and the Parliament in co-decision); PreLex allows the tracking of all parliamentary reports (in full text) based on this proposal.

Earlier work has convincingly argued that it makes sense to control the change from the status quo by focusing only on non-amending legislation (Franchino 2007: 61). Introducing delegation in new acts is substantially different from amending acts that already exist. In the first case, the decision over legislation or delegation (and, if the latter, which committee type to choose) is taken from scratch; in the second, legislation and often also delegation already existed. In other words, the status quo (the position without making a decision), and hence the preferences of the involved actors, are very different in the two cases. We therefore select non-amending proposals only. Furthermore, we focus on binding legal acts of general application (directly or indirectly through member states), i.e. regulations and directives. While we acknowledge that decisions are an important component of European law, as already explained, they are different in the sense that their aim is not to produce law of general applicability.

Several studies have demonstrated that delegation varies both across issue areas and according to the voting rule in the Council (Franchino 2001, 2002, 2004; Pollack 2003; Ch. 2 this vol.). In order to study the possible impact of an increase in parliamentary competences, we selected one article of the treaty under which co-decision was introduced during the period covered by our database while controlling for policy attributes and for the decision-making rule.

We selected Art. 130s(1) TEC (Maastricht)[3] on environmental policy because it is the only treaty article, among those that provide for QMV during the entire period under investigation while changing from cooperation or consultation to co-decision in the Amsterdam Treaty,[4] on which a sizable number of non-amending Commission proposals were based. Environmental issues constitute an important area of European policymaking, both in scope and in their implications for member states (Weale et al. 2000: 1). Additionally, environmental policy has been described as a policy field where the Parliament (and particularly the environmental committee) is pro-active (Burns 2005). Hence, the Commission and the Council may be particularly concerned with possible decision-making gridlocks resulting from the introduction of co-decision in this policy area. Nevertheless, environmental policy is not a 'most likely case' for triggering an increase in delegation after introducing the Parliament as a co-legislator. It should be borne in mind that, in environmental policy, the Treaty of Amsterdam replaced cooperation (and not consultation) by co-decision. This may have generated smaller changes in the frequency of delegation than if consultation had been replaced by co-decision.

Dependent variables

To measure our independent variables, when studying the legislative items based on Arts 130s TEC (Maastricht)/175 TEC (Amsterdam and Nice), we asked:

(i) Does the proposal grant the Commission the power to pass secondary legislation? We identify all proposals including at least one provision enabling the Commission to adopt secondary legislation (delegation proposals). In general, these provisions enable the Commission to pass acts executing or detailing the legislation, to amend non-essential aspects of the law, or even to adopt annexes to it.[5]

(ii) Is the delegation proposal supported by the Council (in its common position) and the Parliament (in its last reading)? In

---

[3] Which became Art. 175 (TEC) Amsterdam.

[4] The Eur-Lex database does not allow us to analyse the changes introduced with the Maastricht Treaty.

[5] Given our focus on the choice between legislating and delegating, we opt for a narrower definition of delegation than that used by Franchino (2001). He defines delegating provisions as 'any major provision that gives...the Commission authority to move the policy away from the status quo' (Franchino 2001: 31), which, for instance, also includes the management of resources and public procurements, etc.

cases where the legislator(s) adopt(s) the proposal but remove(s) the delegating provision, the delegation act was coded as 'not adopted'. We also scrutinized whether the amendments by the legislator(s) provide for a change in the scope of the delegation proposal. In order to measure whether the legislator changes the substantive scope of delegation as originally envisaged in the Commission proposal, we count the number of amendments increasing/decreasing the extent of the substantive areas covered by delegation.[6]

(iii) Which committee(s) was/were proposed by the Commission (in its proposal), the Parliament (in the first reading), and the Council (in the common position)? If two different committees were selected, the proposal was coded twice.[7]

Hence, we measure delegation in a more elaborate fashion than we did in Chapter 3, in which delegation was calculated by dividing the number of Delegated Acts (directives or regulations) passed by the Commission by the total number of directives or regulations passed in a given policy field. As we wrote earlier in Chapter 3, the aims were to describe the overall patterns and trends in legislative activity, and hence rely on broad indicators of delegation and legislation. In this chapter, we go for a more specific procedure to calculate—for a given treaty article— the proportion of legislative proposals including delegation of legislative powers to the European Commission.

As regards the dependent variables, it has to be noted that there are some important differences between our focus and that of the principal– agent theorists. First, we analyse here a more specific type of delegation: the decision to delegate, or not, powers to the Commission *to pass secondary legislation* (in collaboration with committees of member states). For example, we do *not* consider here clauses enabling the Commission to take *non-legislative* decisions in a given area with or without consulting a committee of member states.

A second difference in our approach lies in the type of control mechanisms for the Commission. Whereas many authors include a large variety of control mechanisms (Franchino 2004), it makes sense, theoretically, to focus exclusively on comitology committees. This choice is in line with the literature, which focuses exclusively on comitology procedures, often as *deck-stacking rules,* i.e. those rules ensuring that the

---

[6] For example, if the Parliament or the Council introduce an amendment to specify delegation or eliminate delegating provisions.

[7] It was the case for three proposals only. The legislation can also allow the Commission to take legislative decisions without committees of member states, but we found no such cases in our data collection.

interests of the principal are protected (McCubbins et al. 1987; Brandsma and Blom-Hansen 2011).

Finally, we also include the Commission's preferences for delegation as a dependent variable. In our view, this is crucial to understanding the final legislative outcomes: the Commission's right of initiative in legislation,[8] together with the fact that unanimity is needed to change a Commission proposal, grants the latter considerable influence. Hence, a change in the Commission's preferences regarding delegation also influences the legislative outcome.

Independent variables

As described above, our data collection controls the policy area. It starts in 1994 and ends in June 2006, i.e. just before the revision of the Comitology Decision in 2006. Since our main explanatory variable is the signature of the Amsterdam Treaty, we introduce a dummy variable that takes the value of '0' before October 1997 and '1' after October 1997. We also introduce a dummy variable for the effective introduction of co-decision in May 1999. It must be remembered that this date coincides almost perfectly with the revision of the Comitology Decision (in July 1999). In Chapter 7, we show that this change has an impact on the propensity of the Commission to delegate. That is why the effect of the dummy variable should be considered as the joint effect of the two institutional changes that could not possibly be measured separately with our data.

Although we measure delegation in a different way from how it has been done previously, it still makes a lot of sense to build on the principal–agent theorists' findings when selecting control variables. Indeed, the variables which have been proven to influence the decision to delegate a large variety of discretionary powers are likely to hold true for the decision to delegate powers to pass secondary legislation.

First, we need to control for complexity, as complexity has been proved to be associated with the delegation of large discretionary powers to the Commission (Franchino 2002) and to the member states (Thomson and Torenvlied 2011). While proposals based on the same treaty article will probably require a similar degree of technical expertise, relying on a single treaty base is not sufficient to control one of the most important variables of delegation, namely complexity. This variable is inherently difficult to measure; and relying on proxies runs the risk of measuring something

---

[8] In the last decade this formal rule has—to some extent—been altered by informal practices allowing for legislative initiatives of the European Council and the EP (Rasmussen 2007).

other than complexity.[9] Nevertheless, we introduce the number of repetitions[10] and the number of words as control variables because they have been proved to be correlated with discretion.

We also include a variable to measure the workload per year in environmental policy. The Commission may anticipate circumstances where ministers of the environment have a large number of measures to process and—therefore—would be more willing to accept Commission delegation proposals. As a result, we took the overall number of proposals for legislation based on Arts 130s TEC (Maastricht)/175 TEC (Amsterdam and Nice), which were tabled by the Commission for each year to be accounted for, and computed a variable 'workload' per year.

Additionally, we break delegation down into delegation under directives and delegation under regulations, and control for the use of a particular legislative proposal. We expect to find a difference, since directives leave the transposition and implementation of legislation to member states, while regulations are directly applied by national administrations.

Finally, we control for the number of member states, as an increase in the number and diversity of principals may lead to more delegation (Fiorina 1986; Epstein and O'Halloran 1999). For this purpose, first we simply introduce the number of member states as a continuous variable. However, as this measure may be problematic, since enlargement has not been a continuous process, we additionally run the test with a dummy variable, taking the value of '0' before enlargement to twenty-five member states in May 2004, and '1' afterwards.

6.3 Empirical findings: Does co-decision foster delegation, and if so, what type of delegation?

We use a binary logistic regression to estimate whether the extension of co-decision to environmental policies affects delegation in the Commission proposals, controlling for other predictors. A logistic regression analysis is appropriate here because the dependent variable is a dichotomous variable. The unit of analysis is the individual Commission proposal (n = 71). As our analysis deals with the entire 'population' of proposals in the field of environmental policy, we may therefore choose

---

[9] For example, Franchino considered the number of provisions calling for the adoption of 'detailed rules' as proxy for complexity. However, the requirement of more detailed rules could be an indicator, rather than a cause, of extensive delegation (see Franchino 2007: 146).

[10] i.e. the number of paragraphs starting with 'whereas'.

a higher Alfa level (0.1) as a maximum for significance and, generally speaking, we need not be overly concerned with the significance level but rather focus on its strength.

Table 6.1 presents the results. We observe a positive, strong, and statistically significant relationship between making a proposal of delegation on the one hand, and the fact that this proposal is made after the signing of the Amsterdam Treaty on the other hand. All things being equal, the signing of the Amsterdam Treaty increases the probability that a proposal includes delegation by more than 40. We hence consider our hypothesis *H3* to be confirmed.

We also observe a positive and significant correlation between the number of recitals and the inclusion of delegation in the Commission's proposals: ceteris paribus, every recital increases the odds of delegation by almost 10 per cent. In Model 2, the number of words was included instead, and we again observe a significant and positive relation—so that the odds that the Commission includes delegation in its proposals increases by 2 per cent for each additional 100 words. This suggests that the Commission is more likely to propose delegation when legislation is complex.

In Model 3, we observe that the correlation between delegation in the proposal and the fact that this proposal is made after the signing of the Amsterdam Treaty (i.e. after the introduction of co-decision) is positive (but not significant)—suggesting that the introduction of the Amsterdam Treaty, which also coincides with the revision of the Comitology Decision, gives a supplementary incentive to the Commission to include delegation in its proposal. Quite surprisingly, neither the impact of the annual workload nor the number of member states[11] significantly influences the propensity of the Commission to propose delegation.

Figure 6.1 shows the development of Commission proposals for delegation (out of all proposals) and the development of the percentage of delegation proposals over the total of proposals from 1994 to 2008 (inclusive). What emerges clearly from Figure 6.1 is a very strong increase in the percentage of delegation proposals in the two years following the signing of the Amsterdam Treaty, which is followed by a not so strong and more irregular but nevertheless clear increase after the introduction of the co-decision procedure in 1999.[12] This figure reveals the willingness of the Commission to propose delegation as much as

---

[11] The results are almost identical when the variable 'Number of Member States' is replaced by a dummy variable, taking the value of 0 before the enlargement to the twenty-five new member states and 1 afterwards.

[12] This also coincides with the revision of the 1987 Comitology Decision. See section 6.2 and Chapter 7.

Table 6.1 Factors affecting delegation in the Commission proposal (Articles 130s TEC (Maastricht)/175 TEC [Amsterdam and Nice])

	Model 1		Model 2		Model 3	
	Exp(B) (SE)	Sig	Exp(B) (SE)	Sig	Exp(B) (SE)	Sig
After signature of the Amsterdam Treaty	46.424*** (1.408)	0.006	22.213** (1.264)	0.014	44.092*** (1.442)	0.009
Directive	0.860 (0.595)	0.801	1.060 (0.636)	0.927	0.840 (0.603)	0.773
Number of Recitals (Models 1, 3)	1.098*	0.074	1.022**	0.032	1.114	0.163
Number of hundred words (Model 2)	(0.052)		(0.010)		(0.077)	
Number of member states	1.045 (0.068)	0.516	1.004 (0.070)	0.957	1.041 (0.071)	0.574
Yearly workload	1.055 (0.160)	0.737	0.872 (0.151)	0.366	1.037 (0.174)	0.836
Entry into force of co-decision/1999 Comitology Decision					1.486 (1.519)	0.794
Constant	0.007** (2.183)	0.025	0.041* (1.756)	0.069	0.007** (2.271)	0.027
Nagelkerke R2	0.302		0.387		0.303	
N	71		71		71	

***$p < 0.01$

possible in the period following the signing of the Amsterdam Treaty and preceding the effective introduction of co-decision. Clearly, the Commission seems to have anticipated its incoming loss of power derived from the introduction of co-decision in the environmental area, and rushed to counteract this loss before having to face the Parliament's veto of the decision to delegate. Also, in line with our expectations, the Commission's willingness to propose delegation remains high and even slightly increases in the period following the signing of the Amsterdam Treaty.

The following quotes, from a civil servant in the Directorate-General for Agriculture and Rural Development, after the signature of the constitutional treaty extending co-decision to agriculture, are a good illustration of how the Commission anticipates its future loss of power and the increase in difficulty associated with the European Parliament's stronger role:

We think that with codecision it will be harder to get our proposals passed, yes, that is sure ... I mean, at a certain moment, in the Council you know the member states, you know your colleagues from the management committees. If you go to Parliament, it is completely different. Parliamentarians are not officials, they have other sensibilities. They are organized in other ways, in the Parliament you have political parties.[13]

At the foot of Figure 6.1, we also show the average percentage of delegation proposals per year and the increase in delegation proposals, comparing a first period covering the time before the signing of the Amsterdam Treaty (1997); a second covering the two years between the signing and coming into force of the Treaty, i.e. the period when the Commission knew that co-decision would be introduced in the near future; and a third for the time when co-decision was in force. What emerges is that the average proportion doubled from the first to the second period, rising from 25 per cent to 53 per cent (i.e. by an average yearly increase of 14 per cent), and continued to increase from the second to the third period, although the yearly increase was much smaller (+1.7 per cent).

As regards the Commission's selection of a specific committee, we proposed two alternative hypotheses: with an increasing number of delegation proposals, the Commission will propose the least constraining procedures, i.e. advisory and management committees (*H4*); and, with an increasing number of delegation proposals, the Commission will propose the more restrictive comitology procedure, i.e. regulatory committees (*H IV*).

Figure 6.2 shows the number of delegation proposals for each year, based on Arts 130s TEC (Maastricht)/175 TEC (Amsterdam and Nice), together with the number of proposals delegating to a regulatory committee.[14]

Figure 6.2 clearly supports the second expectation, as it shows a strong link between the increase in delegation proposals and the use of the regulatory procedure starting with the signing of the Amsterdam Treaty in 1997. The proportion of regulatory procedures proposed (out of the total number of procedures) went up from virtually 0 per cent in 1994 to 50 per cent in 1997 and to 100 per cent after 2005. The Commission clearly linked the increase in delegation to proposing the use of regulatory committees, as expected under *H IV*. We also observe that the link between the increase in delegation proposals and the increase in proposals for regulatory committees clearly rose after 1999. In other words, the share of 'regulatory committee' proposals as a proportion of all

---

[13] Interview, the Commission, March 2006.

[14] Our N is the total number of committees introduced in non-amending Commission proposals (regulations and directives) delegating the power to adopt secondary legislation to the Commission.

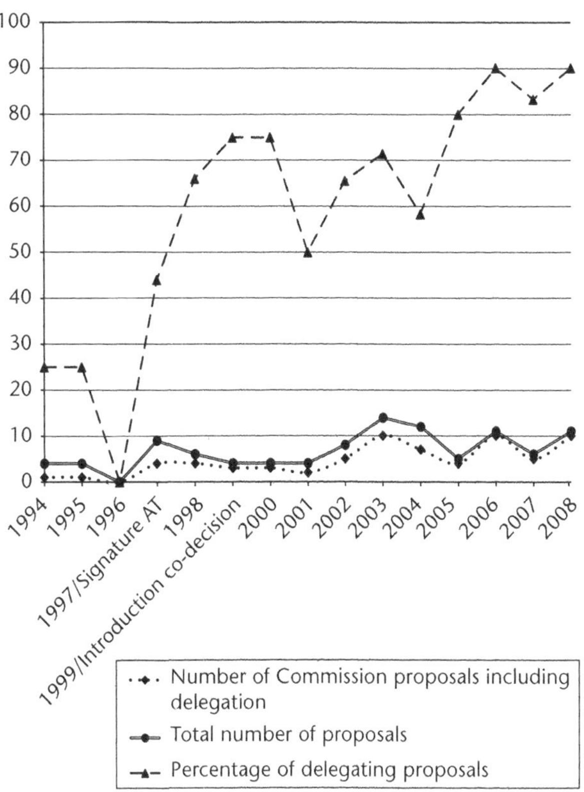

	Before signing of Amsterdam Treaty 1994–1996	After signing of AT but before its entry into force 1997–1999	After introduction of co-decision 2000–2008
Number of Commission proposals including delegation (average)	25.0 per cent	57.9 per cent	73.3 per cent
Average yearly increase		+25.0 per cent	+1.7 per cent

Figure 6.1 Absolute numbers of delegating and non-delegating legislative proposals, and proportion of delegating legislation proposals (per cent); N = 102 proposals

delegation proposals increased significantly from 1999 to 2000 and remains substantial after this date. As we will demonstrate in detail in Chapter 7, this increased willingness of the Commission to use the regulatory procedure rather than the management or advisory commit-tees was additionally supported by the abolition of the *contre-filet*

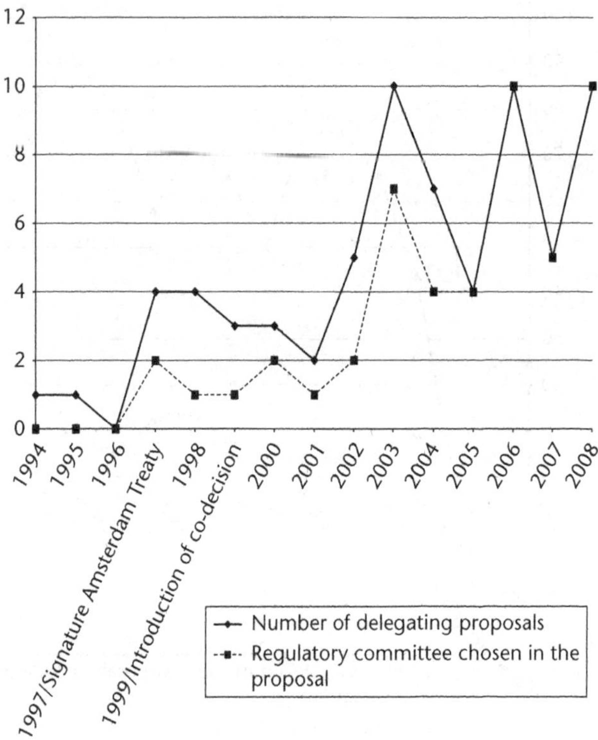

Figure 6.2 Number of delegation proposals and number of regulatory committees chosen; N = 69 proposals

regulatory procedure in July 1999, an institutional change welcomed by the Commission.

In sum, the Commission—anticipating that member states would only be willing to delegate if they maintained control over matters of delegation—imposed greater procedural control on itself while increasing the number of delegation proposals.[15] These results confirm our expectation that if an actor (the Commission) strategically anticipates the contrary preferences of its interacting partner (the Council), it will settle for the second-best solution (more constraining committees) in order to obtain an acceptable outcome (delegation rather than co-decision).

---

[15] This applies especially since the revision of the Comitology Decision in July 1999.

How did the Council react to co-decision, and to what extent did it accept the increase in delegation proposals by the Commission? We hypothesized in *H5* that, with Parliament's increasing legislative competences under co-decision, the Council would be inclined to delegate more to comitology. In order to test this argument, we first scrutinize whether the Commission's proposals for delegation have been more frequently accepted by the Council since the signing of the Amsterdam Treaty than they were prior to that point. Since it takes on average two years to adopt legislation, and in view of the fact that we ended our data collection at the end of 2008, we are looking only at the rate of proposals made before the end of 2006. Our N is the number of delegation proposals adopted by the Commission before the end of 2006 (N = 54). As the numbers are too small to run a regression,[16] we calculated the phi coefficient of correlation between the two variables, 'delegation accepted by the Council' and 'common position adopted after Amsterdam Treaty', for the population of delegation proposals reaching the Council. The coefficient is significant at the 0.001 level and quite strong (+0.532). In short, after the introduction of co-decision, the Commission was much more successful in seeing delegation accepted by the Council.

Figure 6.3 clearly illustrates the coefficient calculated above. It presents the delegation proposals preceding and following the signing of the Amsterdam Treaty and classifies the items according to whether they reached the Council after or before the signing of the Treaty, whether the draft was adopted by the legislator, whether the Council failed to adopt a common position and whether, under co-decision, the draft was rejected by the Parliament or failed in the conciliation committee. As mentioned above, in cases where one (or both) of the legislators adopted the proposal but removed the delegating provision, the delegation act was coded as not being adopted.

It clearly emerges that the delegation proposals which reached the Council before the signing of the Amsterdam Treaty had a much smaller chance of being adopted than the proposals which reached it in the following period. Before 1997, the Council rejected a delegation proposal in four out of the ten cases, while after 1997 it did so in only one out of the forty-four cases.

To summarize, the Council more frequently refused to delegate to the Commission's implementing powers while it held power of veto over

---

[16] For a regression with three predictors, and an alpha level of 0.1, the minimum sample is sixty-two observations. Numbers obtained from a sample size calculator for multiple regression, available at <www.danielsoper.com/statcalc/calc01.aspx>.

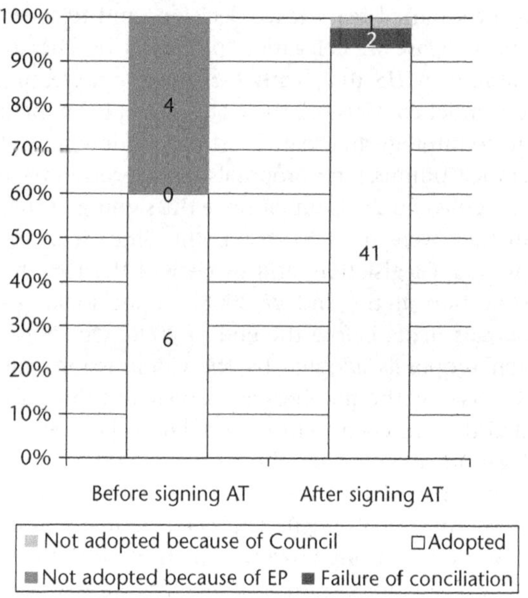

Figure 6.3 The Parliament's and the Council's modification of the Commission's delegation proposals, per type of procedure in use; N = 54

the outcome of the legislative procedure. Once the Parliament was established as a co-legislator under co-decision, the Council increasingly favoured delegation—under which the Parliament had only limited rights until 2006—as opposed to legislation without delegation. Our empirical findings confirm our hypothesis *H5*, and demonstrate that the institutional change that occurred with the introduction of co-decision influenced the preferences of institutional actors for the use of a specific comitology procedure.

In *H6* we argued that the increase in delegation accepted by the Council would be accompanied by an increase in the use of the regulatory committee. In other words, we expected that, with increasing delegation, the Council would wish to delegate only to regulatory committees—in order to maintain control over the Commission. Hence, the increase in delegation following the signing of the Amsterdam Treaty should have led to an increase in the use of regulatory committee procedures.

In Figure 6.4, we present the number of delegation adopted acts based on Arts 130s TEC (Maastricht)/175 TEC (Amsterdam and Nice) and the number of regulatory committees proposed by the Parliament in its first reading and the Council in its common position. Our N is the total number of committees introduced in non-amending adopted acts (regulations and directives) delegating to the Commission the power to adopt secondary legislation.

Unsurprisingly, the Council appears as willing as the Commission to link delegation with the use of the regulatory committee. However, it can also be seen that the Council was already willing to link delegation to the use of regulatory procedures before the signing of the Amsterdam Treaty. This is different from what we found for the Commission. Our results thus oblige us to qualify *H6* as follows. While the Council has obviously been keener to delegate after the signing of the Amsterdam Treaty, and hence keener to rely more extensively on regulatory committees—as *H6* predicted—its preference for delegating to the most 'stringent' committee did not date from the signing of the Amsterdam Treaty, but existed well before that event.

Figure 6.4 shows that the Parliament increasingly supported the regulatory procedure after 1999, even though the competences it obtained under the Second Comitology Decision of 1999 were marginal. Indeed, the Parliament consistently opposed the use of regulatory committees in 1996, 1997, and 1998, but did so to a lesser extent in the following period (only in 50 per cent of cases). This finding questions the assumption made by Franchino (2000) that the Parliament's preferences are closer to those of the Commission than to those of the Council, and that

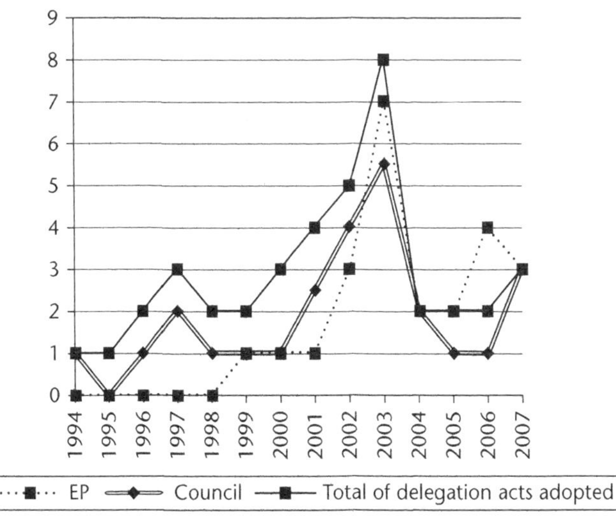

Figure 6.4 Number of delegation adopted acts and number of regulatory committees chosen by the Parliament and the Council; N = 42 delegation acts

it would therefore systematically favour less stringent procedures (see also Pollack 2003).

Another explanation for this surprising finding also reflects the outcome of a bargain between the Parliament and the Council which took place during the negotiations of the 1999 Comitology Decision. The Parliament obtained the suppression of the *contre-filet* mechanism under the regulatory procedure and, in turn, made a concession to stop opposing the regulatory committee procedure (Bergström 2005). Another explanation for the greater willingness to use the regulatory committee after 1999 might be the introduction of co-decision. As observed by Pollack, under the cooperation and consultation procedures, the Parliament 'enjoys the relative luxury of expressing its sincere preferences since its proposals enjoy no special status'.

By contrast, in the co-decision procedure, the Parliament's proposals might 'endanger a fragile majority in the Council' (Pollack 2003: 132). In other words the Parliament, generally eager to adopt legislation expanding the EU's competences, would refrain from opposing the use of the regulatory committee if such self-restraint facilitated the adoption of legislation by the Council.[17] This is the view of a civil servant from Parliament, who noted in 2006 that:

> *The type of committee was a huge issue ten years ago, when we systematically put amendments to change the committee from management or regulatory to the advisory one. It is not anymore, for several reasons. One of these is the right of scrutiny granted to the EP, and the other is the establishment of the co-decision procedure, which gives more influence to the EP over the scope of the original discussion.*

In general, our findings largely suggest that both the Council and the Commission try to circumvent the Parliament through delegation. After the empowerment of the Parliament in legislation, they prefer to adopt secondary legislation via comitology procedures. How did the Parliament react to this behaviour? In *H7* we claimed that: with the introduction of co-decision, the Parliament will seek to veto delegation and press for legislation only.

Surprisingly, our data show that, in the great majority of cases (93 per cent),[18] the EP does not oppose the adoption of delegating legislation under co-decision. Only twice (in twenty-nine cases) did the Parliament (at its first reading) delete the provision allowing the Commission to adopt an

---

[17] However, this explanation is based on a different behavioural assumption, i.e. that actors are driven by efficiency ('policy maximizing') motives.

[18] This refers to the percentage of proposals going to Council under co-decision.

implementing act under co-decision, while it did so once (in fifteen cases) under cooperation. This finding contradicts our *H7*. The Parliament does not appear to be categorically opposed to delegation. Figure 6.5, which presents the types of modification that the Parliament and the Council insert in the Commission's delegation proposals, throws some light on this puzzling finding.

It shows that while the Parliament rarely rejected delegation entirely, it restricted its scope much more frequently under co-decision than it did under cooperation. Under the cooperation procedure, the Parliament either rejected delegation or reduced the substantive extent of delegation as proposed by the Commission in one-third of cases. By contrast, it has done so in almost 70 per cent of cases under the co-decision procedure. It appears, therefore, that the Parliament does not oppose delegation altogether, even if technically it could have done so under the co-decision procedure, but rather opposes delegation of broad scope. This finding obliges us to modify our previous argument. It appears that the

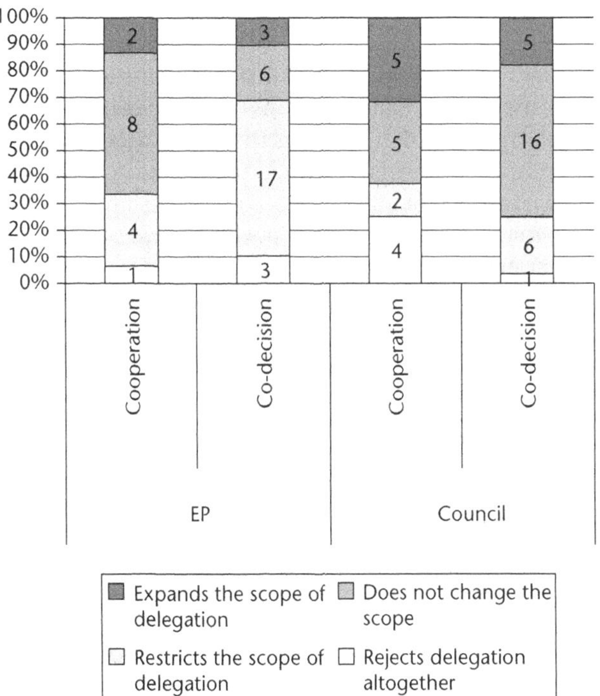

Figure 6.5 The Parliament's and the Council's modification of the Commission's delegation proposals, per type of procedure in use; N = 44

Parliament is willing to support a substantial degree of delegation to the Commission as long as this delegation is—at the same time—restricted in scope. As the EP official cited earlier continues:

> 'What is now the issue is what you leave to comitology or not. We are not interested in the details, we can delegate details to the Commission. But we want to avoid sensitive issues being left to comitology, because once it is delegated, it is gone for ever'

Finally, we also observe in Figure 6.5 that while the Council is much less willing to reject delegation under co-decision than under the cooperation procedure, it is also slightly more willing under co-decision to restrict the scope of delegation (and less willing to extend this scope). This supports the conclusion that, although the Council is prepared to increasingly delegate to the Commission since the introduction of co-decision, it is also careful not to delegate without strings attached.

6.4 Conclusion

In this chapter, we test a distributive institutionalist argument of why and how a change of distribution of power through institutional change affects the balance of power between the EU institutional actors and thereby affects actors' preferences either to legislate on a given matter or to delegate the issue to comitology. Based on the assumption that actors seek to maximize their institutional power in order to increase their influence over policy outcomes, we argue that the treaty-based obligation to share legislative power with the Parliament motivates both the Council and the Commission to try to circumvent the Parliament through delegation by proposing and adopting secondary legislation in comitology procedures. As a consequence, we expect that the Parliament will react by opposing the use of delegation.

We first show that, in environmental policy, the Commission and the Council have indeed been more willing to rely on extensive delegation since the extension of co-decision in this field. The increase in delegation in the two years following the signing of the Amsterdam Treaty indicates that the Commission and the Council anticipated a relative loss of power to the Parliament and rushed to delegate as much as possible to the Commission before the effective introduction of co-decision. However, the Council was only willing to delegate more to the Commission on condition that it could exert as much control as possible over the procedure by using regulatory committees—a condition that the Commission strategically anticipates in its delegation proposals. As for the Parliament, we expected that the introduction of co-decision would lead to it opposing delegation altogether. This expectation was not confirmed. It emerges that the Parliament does not oppose delegation as such, but rather systematically restricts its scope.

7

The impact of the 1999 Comitology Decision: Agricultural and taxation policy

In the preceding chapter we demonstrated that the Commission and the Council were clearly more willing to rely on delegation in the environmental field once they knew co-decision would be extended to this policy. Here, we focus on a second change of an institutional rule, a rule governing comitology itself, in order to analyse the consequences of the rule change on actors' preferences. Building again on distributive bargaining theory, we expect that the preferences of actors regarding whether or not to delegate will also depend on their competences under *delegation*.

To test that argument, we focus on the change of actors' preferences which resulted from the Comitology Decision of 1999—a reform that responded to the Commission's long quest for the abolition of the 'double safety net' mechanisms.[1] Since the EP's preferences have been examined in depth in the preceding chapter, we analyse a policy area subject to consultation and concentrate only on the change of preferences of the Commission and the Council.[2]

7.1 Hypotheses

In line with our theoretical perspective, we build on J. Knight's (1992) distributive bargaining theory and expect that the preferences of actors regarding whether or not to delegate will depend on their competences under delegation. As detailed in Chapter 2, we

---

[1] Proposal for a Council Decision laying down the procedures for the exercise of implementing powers conferred on the Commission (98/C 279/05) COM(1998) 380 final—98/0219(CNS).

[2] Part of the empirical analysis has been previously published in Moury and Héritier (2013).

expect that if the procedures governing delegation are changed so as to alter the distribution of competences, actors will modify their preferences for delegation accordingly. The actor(s) who gained competences under delegation will increasingly opt for delegation, whereas the actor(s) who suffered a relative loss in competences will not choose delegation.

After the Comitology Decision of July 1999, the Commission increased its chances of having its favourite legislative outcome passed in management and regulatory committees. We consequently expected that the Commission would have been keener after July 1999 to propose delegation under these committees for acts that could alternatively be adopted by legislation or with advisory procedures. Additionally, it might be argued that the Commission anticipates the Council's opposition to the use of management procedures for Delegated Acts that could alternatively be adopted through legislation or with a regulatory committee.[3] We therefore expect that although the Commission was more willing to delegate to management committees after 1999 than before, it would refrain from proposing this committee too frequently.

By contrast, in regulatory committees—in which member states have maximum control, the Commission is less likely to anticipate resistance. In other words, we expect that the Commission delegated more frequently to both regulatory and management committees after the adoption of the Second Comitology Decision, but more so to regulatory than to management committees.

Finally, whereas member states in the Council suffered a relative loss of influence in comitology with the 1999 Decision, their influence in legislation remained untouched. In other words, in July 1999 it became more difficult for member states to obtain their favourite legislative outcome in management and regulatory committees. In a similar reasoning as expressed above, we expect the Council—willing to protect its own institutional power—to resist the attempts of the Commission to delegate greater implementing powers to management and regulatory committee after the Second Comitology Decision.

---

[3] The probable objection of the Council to the advisory and management committees may be derived from the Council's Comitology Decision, which states that regulatory committees should be used in the case of 'measures of general scope designed to apply essential provisions of basic instruments' and to the updating or adaptation of 'certain non-essential provisions of the instrument'.

We therefore submit:

H8 After the adoption of the Second Comitology Decision, the Commission more frequently proposed delegation of implementing powers under the regulatory and management procedures.

H9 After the adoption of the Second Comitology Decision, the increase in proposals delegated by the Commission to Regulatory committees is higher than those delegated to Management Committees.

H10 After the adoption of the Second Comitology Decision, the Council would more frequently reject Commission delegation proposals to management and regulatory committees.

7.2 Databases

In line with our previous choices, we rely on a database using the EU online catalogue. A second database, examining the EP's amendments to Commission proposals during the consultation procedure (across all policy sectors), is built to illustrate *H8* and *H9* from a different perspective.

7.2.1 *Commission proposals (agriculture and taxation)*

Similar to the procedure followed for the environmental policy, we first built a database using the EU's EUR-Lex online catalogue, which allows us to scrutinize the full text of all Commission proposals based on a given treaty article and to identify the resulting final legislation adopted by the Council (since 1994). In order to isolate the possible impact of the 1999 Comitology Decision, and to control for the issue area and the legislative procedure, we selected two articles of the treaty under which neither the legislative procedure nor the voting rule in the Council changed during the period of time under study, namely Art. 43 on agricultural policy (QMV, consultation) and Arts 99 and 100 on taxation (unanimity, consultation). These three specific articles were chosen because they were the only ones subject to the same decision-making rules (from January 1994 to March 2008) on which a sizable number of Commission proposals were based. Just as in the case of the proposals on the environment, we focus on non-amending proposals for regulations and directives.

DEPENDENT VARIABLES
In scrutinizing the legislative items based on Arts 45, 99, and 100, we ask the same questions as in Chapter 4, with the exception of those on the Parliament's preferences, which were omitted. Thus we ask: (1) Does the

proposal include the delegation of legislative powers to the Commission? (2) Is the delegation proposal supported by the Council in the final act?[4] (3) Which committee(s) was/were put forward by the Commission in its proposal, and which were adopted by the Council in the final act?[5]

INDEPENDENT VARIABLES

As described above, our data collection controls for policy area and for the rule of legislative procedure: consultation and QMV for agriculture; and consultation and unanimity for taxation. As the revision of the Comitology Decision in 2006 has no impact on legislative acts adopted on the basis of the consultation procedure, the only institutional change for the policy area selected during the period under study (1994–2008) was the 1999 Comitology Decision. We therefore introduced a dummy variable, taking the value of *0* in the period preceding July 1999, and *1* afterwards.

As in Chapter 5, we introduce the following control variables: 'the number of words', 'the number of recitals', the 'workload per year', the 'number of member states'; and we break delegation down into delegation under directives and delegation under regulations. We also control for the diversity of preferences of the Council and the Commission. While Franchino (2004) measures the divergence by counting the number of amendments the Council introduced in the Commission proposals, we focus on the percentage of paragraphs amended by the Council in the final text.[6] We then compute a categorical variable running from *0* (both texts are identical) to 100 (when every paragraph is amended or when the delegation proposal is never adopted).[7]

As the Comitology Decision took place only a few months before the new Commission term of Prodi (September 1999), and since it might be argued that a new Commission would be willing to delegate as much as possible at the beginning of its term,[8] we introduce a dummy taking the

---

[4] The Council removes the delegating clause in nine delegation proposals and adds one in twelve Commission proposals. In these cases, respectively, the delegating act was considered as not having been adopted; and a delegation proposal is counted as proposed and passed.

[5] If two different committees were selected, the proposal was codified twice. This was the case for 11 proposals (of the 333 proposals).

[6] On average, 54.5 per cent of articles are amended. The standard variation of this variable is 20.7 per cent and the range 81 per cent.

[7] From our database we calculated that the average time for passing delegation based on Article 43 was 1 year and 6 months. We therefore examined whether proposals made by the Commission up to June 2008 had been passed or not passed by the Council by December 2009. If not, we assigned the value of 100.

[8] No proposals were made by the resigning Santer Commission (March–September 1999).

form of *1* when the legislation is proposed in the first year of a Commission term and *0* otherwise.

Finally, we introduce a dummy variable for the signature of the Lisbon Treaty in December 2007 (taking the value of *0* before this date and *1* afterwards). As we know, the treaty introduced co-decision for agricultural matters[9] once it entered into force in December 2009. In the preceding chapter, we showed that in this case the Commission anticipated its future loss of power to the EP and rushed to propose as much delegation to itself as possible, especially in the period following the signature of the treaty and preceding its entry into force.

7.2.2 *All parliamentary reports on consultation*

We complement this first database with a second one, based on parliamentary online archives (Legislative Observatory—OEIL) that include all parliamentary reports from the same period (1994–2008). We scrutinized all legislative reports deposited by the EP[10] during the *consultation* procedure that amended the Commission proposal for directives. The reason for presenting these data is that they are a good illustration of the increase in the Commission's propensity to delegate to itself after 1999. Indeed, if such an attempt was to be confirmed, it should also be visible in the reluctance of the Parliament to allow increasing delegation—a procedure in which it is not even consulted. Applying a keyword search,[11] we selected reports which introduced at least one amendment aimed at restricting the scope of implementing powers delegated to the Commission. In order to increase the number of cases, we focused on *all* issue areas. We compared the number of reports including restricting amendments with the total number of reports commenting on proposals for directives. Our data collection started with the reports for 1994 when data became available from the EP Internet site and extended to the end of 2007.

---

[9] The same reasoning could not be made about the Constitutional Treaty, which had been rejected by a referendum in France and in the Netherlands only six months after its signature.

[10] http://www.europarl.europa.eu/activities/plenary/ta/search.do?language=EN.

[11] More specifically, we identified the reports based on Commission proposals, by selecting reports registering key words such as 'comitology', 'commitology', 'council decision', 'committee', and 'implementation'.

7.3 Empirical findings: The 1999 Comitology Decision spurring delegation

7.3.1 *Agriculture*

Our first two hypotheses focus on the Commission's preferences for delegation, while the third examines those of the Council. To test *H8*, we use a binary logistic regression to estimate whether the 1999 Comitology Decision affects delegation to management and regulatory committees in the Commission proposals, controlling for other predictors. The unit of analysis is the individual proposal (n = 333). As mentioned, our data collection controls for the policy area (and hence indirectly for the complexity of the issue) and the legislative rule (QMV and consultation). Inter-correlation across independent variables

Table 7.1 Binary logistic Regression for delegation to management or regulatory committee in the Commission proposal (Article 43)

	Model 1		Model 2	
	Exp(B) (S.E.)	Sig	Exp(B) (S.E.)	Sig
After Comitology Decision	4.756*** (0.382)	0.000	4.843*** (0.377)	0.000
Signature Lisbon Treaty	4.900*** (0.536)	0.003	4.808*** (0.533)	0.003
Directive	4.181*** (0.402)	0.000	4.080*** (0.403)	0.000
Number of Recitals (Model 1)/Number of hundred words (Model 2)	0.990 (0.009)	0.301	1.003* (0.002)	0.082
Number of member states	1.002 (0.033)	0.948	0.995 (0.033)	0.876
Yearly workload	0.961* (0.022)	0.065	0.960* (0.022)	0.060
First Year of Commission term	0.592 (0.505)	0.300	0.559 (0.501)	0.247
Amendments	0.993 (0.005)	0.223	0.993 (0.005)	0.178
Constant	0.800 (0.819)	0.785		
Year			0.740 (0.805)	0.709
Nagelkerke R2	*0.293*		*0.300*	
N	*333*		*333*	

***p < 0.01
** p < 0.05
* p < 0.1

was tested so that we could be confident about the absence of perfect collinearity across control variables.[12]

As we can see in Table 7.1, the institutional changes (the introduction of the Comitology Decision in July 1999 and the signature of the Amsterdam Treaty in December 2007) have the most significant influence on delegation to management and regulatory committee. The introduction of the Comitology Decision in 1999 and the signature of the Lisbon Treaty increase the odds of delegation by almost five times (ceteris paribus). Moreover, these measurements are statistically significant at the 0.001 and 0.003 level (respectively)—which shows the consistency of the correlation in the population. In view of the above findings, we consider *H8* to be confirmed.

Table 7.1 also shows that proposals for a directive are, on average, more than four times more likely to include delegation to management or regulatory committees (Exp(B) = 4.18, significance = 0.001). This result is surprising, since we have seen in Chapter 3 that there is a higher proportion of delegated regulations than of directives (out of all Delegated Acts) in the field of agriculture. In other words, legislated (i.e. Council and Parliament) directives are more likely than regulations to include a clause delegating the decision-making power of the Commission; but ultimately there are still more delegated (i.e. Commission) regulations than directives. This suggests that legislated directives are likely to be the legal basis for delegated regulations (rather than directives) and/or that a legislated regulation will engender a larger number of delegated acts than a legislated directive.

The results for the proxies for complexity are quite mixed. On the one hand, the number of recitals does not increase the odds of delegation in the Commission proposal; but on the other hand, each additional 100 words increases the odds of delegation by only 0.3 per cent. This shows a very small—but extremely consistent—effect of the length of legislation on delegation. The impact of the yearly workload is significant, but also very small and negative rather than positive as we might have expected. Finally, neither the number of member states,[13] the beginning of the Commission terms, the percentage of paragraphs amended, nor the year seem to influence the propensity of the Commission to propose delegation.[14]

---

[12] The yearly workload and the first year of the Commission term are not very strongly correlated (Pearson's R = −.326) and hence could be inserted together in the regression without violating the assumptions.

[13] The results are almost identical when the variable 'Number of member states' is replaced by a dummy variable taking the value of *0* before the enlargement to the twenty-five new member states and *1* afterwards.

[14] We also introduced the year as a control variable to check for an effect of a mere temporal trend on delegation. Doing so, the Exp(B) coefficient of the variable 'introduction

Figure 7.1 Frequency of Commission proposals delegating implementing power to management and regulatory committees and Percentage of Commission proposals delegating implementing power to management and regulatory committees, N = 395 proposals

	Before 1999 Comitology Decision	*After 1999 Comitology Decision*
Percentage of Commission proposals including delegation to management or regulatory committees (absolute number)	15.8 per cent (24/152)	57.1 per cent (140/245)
Percentage of Commission proposals *for Directives* including delegation to management or regulatory committees (absolute number)	22.7 per cent (5/22)	78.6 per cent (33/42)
Percentage of Commission proposals *for Regulations* including delegation to management or regulatory committees (absolute number)	14.6 per cent (19/130)	52.7 per cent (107/203)

Table 7.2 Factors affecting the use of the regulatory committee in the Commission proposal (Article 43, reference: non-delegation)

| | | Exp (B) | |
		(S.E.)	(Sig.)
Advisory	Intercept	(1.757)	0.258
	After Comitology Decision	1.108	0.903
		(0.845)	
	Signature Lisbon Treaty	1.268	0.860
		(1.351)	
	Number of Member States	1.001	0.990
		(0.083)	
	Directive	8.964***	0.001
		(0.653)	
	Number of Recitals	0.997	0.856
		(0.017)	
	Yearly Workload	0.992	0.839
		(0.042)	
	Amendments	0.988	0.322
		(0.012)	
	N	16	
Management	Intercept	(0.943)	0.296
	After Comitology Decision	3.913***	0.001
		(0.430)	
	Signature Lisbon Treaty	5.482***	0.005
		(0.606)	
	Number of Member States	0.961	0.295
		(0.037)	
	Directive	3.447**	0.015
		(0.511)	
	Number of Recitals	0.974	0.176
		(0.020)	
	Yearly Workload	0.956**	0.047
		(0.023)	
	Amendments	0.986**	0.022
		(0.006)	
	N	87	
Regulatory	Intercept	(1.354)	0.001
	After Comitology Decision	8.644**	0.004
		(0.743)	
	Signature Lisbon Treaty	2.485	0.168
		(0.660)	
	Number of Member States	1.048	0.339
		(0.049)	
	Directive	11.905***	0.000
		(0.527)	
	Number of Recitals	0.996	0.787
		(0.013)	
	Yearly Workload	0.997	0.928
		(0.032)	
	Amendments	1.003	0.706
		(0.008)	

N	*51*
Nagelkerke R2	*0.343*
N	*335*

The reference category is: non-delegation
***p < 0.01
** p < 0.05
* p < 0.1

Figure 7.1 illustrates the above-mentioned findings. It shows the development of Commission proposals delegating to management and regulatory committees (out of all proposals) based on Art. 45 (agriculture, QMV, consultation) in the periods before and after the adoption of the Comitology Decision in 1999.

While the Commission seems, indeed, to have been increasingly willing to propose delegation since 1993, we observe a very strong increase in the percentage of delegation proposals from 1998 to 1999 (+45 per cent), which gradually decreased until 2002 (to a level which remains nevertheless higher than before 1999). Thereafter, the proportion of delegation proposals gradually increases again up to a spectacular 81 per cent in 2008, i.e. in the year following the signature of the Lisbon Treaty and preceding its entry into force.

What emerges from Figure 7.1 is the Commission's clear 'enthusiasm' to delegate to management and regulatory committees in 1999, immediately after the introduction of the Comitology Decision. A Commission official explains this 'enthusiasm' by the fact that, in the period immediately following a change to a rule, the choice of a particular procedure is often more 'political' (in the sense of fighting for power) than 'legal' (in the sense of finding which committees are legally appropriate). After a while, the 'legal' arguments regain importance, albeit without cancelling the political motivations:

> Just after the comitology change of 1999, the debate about which procedure to choose was mainly political, not legal, in that the choice between procedures was based on the wish of each actor involved to maximize its institutional power. After a while, we managed to depoliticize debate, so that the battle for power was played down to some extent to the benefit of legality.[15]

of Comitology Decision' decreases to 3.5 (rather than 4.7), but stays significant at the 0.05 level (see Appendix 3).

[15] Interview with an official of the Commission Legal Service, January 2011, own translation from French.

At the foot of Figure 7.1, we also show the average percentage of delegation proposals per year and the increase in delegation proposals, comparing a first period from before the 1999 Comitology Decision to the period after the new decision was in force. In addition, we break down directives and regulations. What appears is that the average proportion for the second period is more than four times higher than in the first, rising from 16 per cent to almost 60 per cent. The increase is striking for both directives and regulations, although a larger proportion of directives include delegation in both periods.

As regards the Commission's selection of a specific committee, we proposed in *H9* that, after the adoption of the Second Comitology Decision, the increase in Commission proposals delegating to regulatory committees would be higher than those delegating to management committees. To test this hypothesis, we use a Multinominal Logistic Regression.[16] This analysis allows for a reference category (no delegation) to be compared with three other categories (delegation to an advisory, management, and regulatory committee). Of the 333 Commission proposals, 16 (5 per cent) delegate to an Advisory Procedure, 87 (26 per cent) to a management procedure, and 51 (15 per cent) to a regulatory procedure. Table 7.3 confirms that the introduction of the Comitology Decision in July 1999 had and still has a significant influence on delegation to management and regulatory committees, and shows that it has no impact on delegation to advisory committees.[17] As expected, the introduction of the Comitology Decision increases the odds of delegation to a *regulatory* committee to a much greater extent than it increases the odds of delegation to a *management* committee (by 8.6 versus 3.9, respectively). This is consistent with our expectation that the Commission sometimes anticipates member states' resistance to increased delegation to management committee and thus more frequently proposes regulatory committees for measures that could alternatively be passed by legislation.

Interestingly, Table 7.2 also shows that the type of proposal (directives rather than regulation) is a significant determinant of delegation in the proposal for all three categories.

In *H10*, we turn to the Council preferences and ask whether the Council would oppose the Commission's attempts to delegate to a greater extent. We submitted that *After the adoption of the Second Comitology Decision, the Council would more frequently reject Commission delegation proposals to management and regulatory committees.*

---

[16] We are obliged to Fabio Franchino for this suggestion.

[17] The results for the advisory committee should be taken with some caution, given the limited number (sixteen) of cases.

Table 7.3 Proportion of proposals which are passed by the Council (N = 364)

	Adopted		Total proposals
	Before Comitology Decision 1999	*After Comitology Decision 1999*	
Proposals that delegate to management or regulatory committees	21/24 (87.5%)	89/97 (91.8%)	110/121 (90.9%)
Proposals that do not delegate to management or regulatory committees	97/118 (82.2%)	111/125 (88.8%)	208/243 (85.6%)
Total	118/142 (83.1%)	200/222 (90.1%)	364

We first examine whether the Commission's proposals for delegation were accepted by the Council less frequently after the adoption of the 1999 Comitology Decision. In Table 7.3, we observe the outcome of Commission proposals and classify the items according to whether or not the proposal was passed by the Council before or after the Comitology Decision, and whether or not it included delegation to management or regulatory committees. As mentioned above, the proposal is codified as being rejected when the Council passes the delegation proposals but removes the clause allowing for delegation.[18]

Contrary to our expectations, the delegation proposals were adopted by the Council no less frequently after 1999 than before. Quite the contrary; a larger percentage of delegation proposals were passed by the Council after 1999 than prior to it (91.8 per cent versus 87.5 per cent). Moreover, we observe that, on average, delegation proposals have a *greater* chance of being passed by the Council than do non-delegation proposals (90.9 per cent versus 85.6 per cent).

To test *H10*, we then use a binary logistic regression to check whether the 1999 Comitology Decision affects the Council's propensity to pass a proposal delegating to management and regulatory committees. We consider all Commission proposals based on Art. 43, delegating to either a regulatory or a management committee.[19] The dependent variable is a dummy taking the value of *1* when the Council passes the proposal without removing the delegation clause and *0* otherwise. As mentioned above, the proposal is codified as being rejected when the Council passes

---

[18] From our database, we calculated that the average time for passing delegation based on Art. 43 is 1 year and 6 months. We therefore examined whether or not proposals made by the Commission up to June 2008 had been passed by the Council by December 2009.

[19] And is therefore lower than in Tables 7.1 and 7.2, where the population was made up of all Commission proposals.

Table 7.4 Factors affecting the adoption by the Council of a proposal delegating to a management or to a regulatory committee

	Model		Model 2	
	Exp(B) SE	*Sig*	*Exp(B)* SE	*Siq*
After Comitology Decision	0.301	0.373	0.290	0.366
	(1.351)		(1.369)	
Workload per year	1.046	0.287	1.044	0.311
	(0.042)		(0.042)	
Number of MS	1.129**	0.038	1.128**	0.039
	(0.058)		(0.059)	
Directive	0.754	0.718	0.601	0.546
	(0.782)		(0.843)	
Number of recitals	1.353	0.238	1.372	0.236
	(0.256)		(0.267)	
Regulatory			1.553	0.466
			(0.604)	
Constant	0.233	0.451	0.228	0.450
	(1.932)		(1.957)	
Nagelkerke R2	*0.212*		*0.217*	
N	136		136	

***p<0.01
** p<0.05
* p< 0.1

the delegation proposals but removes the clause allowing for delegation.[20] Hence, while the two preceding regression tables examine the variables influencing the odds that the Commission will propose delegation, Table 7.5 looks at the odds of the Council passing these delegation proposals.

In accordance with earlier choices, the yearly workload of the Agriculture Council, the number of member states, the nature of the proposal as a directive, and the number of recitals were inserted in the regression as control variables. In Model 1, we merge the management and regulatory committee; and in Model 2 we introduce another dummy variable to observe whether the Council would behave differently if the Commission proposal delegated to a regulatory committee.

Table 7.4 shows that the introduction of the 1999 Comitology decision reduces the Council's propensity to pass delegating proposals to management or regulatory committees; but that this effect is not convincing in terms of statistical significance. This result does not enable us

---

[20] From our database we calculated that the average time for passing delegation based on Art. 43 was 1 year and 6 months. We therefore examined whether or not proposals made by the Commission up to June 2008 had been passed by the Council by December 2009.

Table 7.5 Proportion of proposals which are passed by the Council (N = 364)

	Adopted		
	Before Comitology Decision 1999	After Comitology Decision 1999	Total proposals
Proposals that delegate to management or regulatory committees	*21/24* *(87.5%)*	*89/97* *(91.8%)*	*110/121* *(90.9%)*
Proposals that do not delegate to management or regulatory committees	*97/118* *(82.2%)*	*111/125* *(88.8%)*	*208/243* *(85.6%)*
Total	*118/142* *(83.1%)*	*200/222* *(90.1%)*	*364*

to confirm *H10*, and shows that the effect of the change in the institutional rule on actors' willingness to delegate significantly holds for the Commission only. This could be explained by two factors. First, if the Council has a strong preference for a policy change and/or is under time constraints to adopt a specific legislative item (bearing unanimity requirements in mind),[21] it may prefer not to oppose the Commission on the question of comitology. Second, while the gain in power induced by the comitology change is obvious for the Commission, the loss of power for the Council is not so straightforward. Indeed, it is not the ministers who are members of the committees, but experts who represent the member states. In other words, the Council's loss of influence is more indirect than the Commission's gain.

As regards the control variables, we observe that only one of them significantly determines the probability of the Council passing a delegation proposal: the number of member states. This *decreases* the probability that a delegation proposal is passed by the Council. More specifically, the addition of one single member state increases the probability that the Council would pass Commission proposals delegating to management or regulatory committees by 13 per cent. This supports the theoretical argument that a divided Council with many members would tend to delegate more to avoid deadlocks on controversial issues.

---

[21] Under the legislative procedure, unanimity is required when the Council amends the proposal in a way that is not supported by the Commission.

7.3.2 *Taxation policy and approximation of laws affecting the common market*

How does our hypothesis claiming a link between the 1999 Comitology Decision and an increasing use of delegation fare in a policy area that has always been subject to the unanimity rule? Not many articles of the treaty remain that provide for unanimous voting in the Council, and a very small number of legislative acts are passed on the articles. We selected Arts 93 and 94 EC (previously 99 and 100 under the Maastricht Treaty, and now Arts 113 and 115 TFEU) because they are the articles under which the unanimity rule applied during the whole period studied, and twenty-nine Commission proposals are based on them. Art. 93 EC related to certain aspects of indirect taxation, and Art. 94 EC concerned the approximation of laws that affect the establishment or functioning of the common market (when Art. 100a EC—now Art. 114 TFEU—was not applicable).

As Figure 7.2 shows, very few proposals are based on these articles, and fewer still call for delegation (only twenty-nine proposals in total, eight of which include delegation). These numbers do not allow us to control for a variety of variables in statistical models, and hence to draw solid conclusions for the taxation sub-field. We nevertheless present them to illustrate that what has been observed for an area subject to QMV is similar to another area subject to unanimity. We also observe in this policy area a clear increase in the proportion of delegation proposals after 1999—a proportion which decreased slightly after 2000 but nevertheless remained higher than before 1999. Again, and despite the very small numbers, the graph indicates a certain eagerness by the Commission to rely on delegation after the introduction of the 1999 Comitology Decision. At the foot of Figure 7.3, we also show the average percentage of delegation proposals per year and the increase in delegation proposals, comparing a first period covering the time before the 1999 Comitology Decision with the period after the new decision entered into force. It shows that the average proportion increased considerably from the first to the second period, rising from 19 to 31 per cent.

As regards the type of committee chosen, the delegation proposals made under these two articles are too few to test our hypothesis: the Commission only submitted eight delegation proposals, i.e. one advisory committee procedure (2005), three management committee procedures (one in 1995, two in 1997) and four regulatory committee procedures (one in 2002, three in 2006). It is interesting to note that half of the committee procedures chosen are regulatory committee procedures, and that all of these were adopted after July 1999. Again, however, these numbers are too small to support any conclusions.

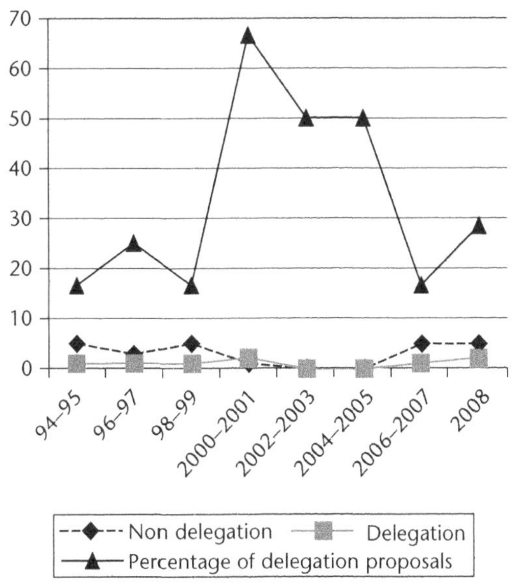

	Before 1999 Comitology Decision	After 1999 Comitology Decision
Number of Commission proposals including delegation (average)	3/16 18.8%	5/16 31.3%

Figure 7.2 Evolution of Commission delegation proposals based on Articles 93 and 94, N = 29

If we look (Table 7.6) at the rate of success these proposals have when they arrive at the Council's table, we find that they did not fare very well. More specifically, only half (fourteen) of the proposals were adopted by the Council out of a total of twenty-nine proposals made before the end of 2006. Delegation and non-delegation proposals reveal the same rate of success, and, as for agriculture, we do not observe any indication that the Council was less willing to adopt delegation proposals after 1999 than it was before.

The rarity of delegating legislation in the area of taxation is consistent with the findings of Epstein and O'Halloran (1999b), that legislators do not wish to delegate powers in the sphere of taxation because they want to reserve the possibility of distributing concentrated benefits to their constituents for themselves. It also supports Franchino's (2001) finding (that member states allow the Commission less discretion in fields subject to the unanimity rule). However, as observed by Pollack (2003: 103), this

Table 7.6 Proportion of proposals which are passed by the Council (N = 29)[22]

	Non-delegation	Delegation
Before July 1999	5/10	3/6
	50%	50%
After July 1999	4/8	3/5
	50%	60%
Total	9/18	6/11
	50%	54.5%

link between unanimity and less discretion is unclear. One possible explanation is that member states retain unanimity in areas which are more sensitive because of national sovereignty issues. In this case, both variables are the effect of a single cause, namely, political sensitivity linked to national sovereignty concerns. Alternatively, the decision rule itself may exert an independent effect, insofar as under QMV a single member state is unable to oppose delegation to the Commission.

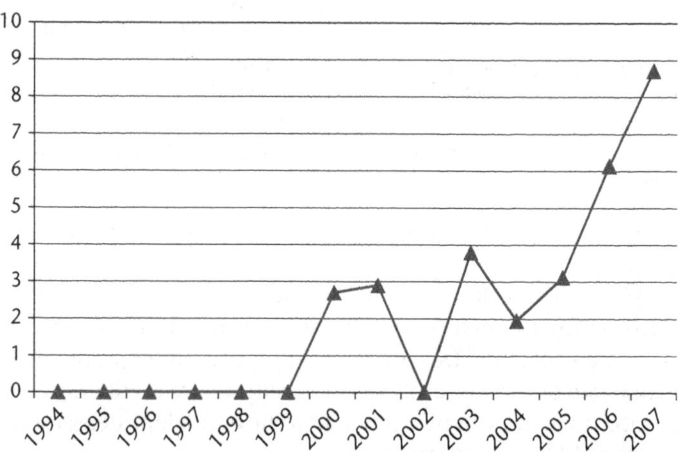

Figure 7.3 Percentage of parliamentary reports on directives (consultation) including at least one amendment to restrict the scope of delegation to the Commission, N = 1029 reports

[22] Given the average time that it takes to pass legislation, we only look at proposals that have been passed by the Commission before 2006.

7.3.3 *EP amendments (all proposals on consultation procedure)*

In order to analyse our findings from a different empirical angle, we used our second database. As expressed below, this database considers parliamentary reports on a Commission proposal for a directive that should be passed by the consultation procedure *across all policy areas* (and thus not only agriculture). Although the proportion of legislative reports of the Parliament restricting the scope of delegation in the Commission proposal is very small (2 per cent on average), it clearly emerges—as expected—that the Parliament started to introduce amendments reducing the scope of delegation from 1999 onwards, with a continuous increase since then. Figure 7.3 therefore brings additional support to our hypothesis that the Commission increasingly delegated to itself following the Comitology Decision of July 1999.

7.4 Conclusion

In this chapter, we test an institutionalist power-based bargaining argument of why the Commission would be increasingly willing to delegate decision-making power to management and regulatory committees after 1999, and why the contrary was to be expected for the Council. We expected that the gain in competences in the regulatory and management committees vis-à-vis the Council would induce the Commission to increasingly propose delegation to these committees. Conversely, we also anticipated that the Council would be less inclined to delegate to these committees after July 1999. In general terms, we argued that a change in the distribution of competences between the EU bodies would affect their preferences to legislate or delegate accordingly.

Our results clearly support our hypothesis for the Commission: controlling for alternative explanations, the Commission is more than four times more likely to delegate to management or regulatory committees since the revision of the 1999 Comitology Decision. Moreover, the effect of the revision of this rule is twice as strong for the regulatory committees. This confirms our expectation that the Commission sometimes strategically refrains from delegating to the management committee measures which could alternatively be adopted through legislation. We also show that the Commission was more willing to rely on extensive delegation once it knew that co-decision would be introduced; a finding we have already illustrated in the preceding chapter.

Another relevant finding is that the level of conflict between the Commission and the Council (measured by the proportion of proposals amended by the Council) or in the Council (measured by the number of member states) does not seem to influence delegation in the Commission proposal—either because the Commission is not able to anticipate it or because the relationship between conflict and delegation, as claimed by Thomson and Torenvlied (2011), is not straightforward.

Another crucial finding is the fact that proposals for directives in particular are more likely to include delegation (to all three committees). Future research should investigate this relationship, which is counterintuitive, since directives allow member states to choose the instruments for implementing the legislative act. What this finding suggests is that delegation to member states converges with, rather than replaces, delegation to the Commission.

Contrary to our expectations, the Council did not increasingly oppose delegation after 1999. What appears to matter to the Council's decision to accept, or alternatively to oppose delegation as proposed by the Commission, is the number of its members—hence bringing some support to the idea that diversity and conflict influence delegation. This difference could be accounted for by the fact that member states—and not the Council—are directly represented in the comitology committees (hence making the loss of influence more indirect in the Council after a comitology reform).

Finally, we observe much less delegation in areas governed by unanimity, where legislative initiatives are more sensitive and where a single member state can block delegation. In this regard, the attempts of the Commission, in connection with the 1999 Comitology Decision, to grant more implementing power 'to itself' were for the most part unsuccessful. This is not surprising: the policy areas still ruled by unanimity are areas where at least some states do not want to delegate policymaking and lawmaking to the supranational level.

8

Conclusion

In this book we have dealt with the following questions: 'Why did the rules governing delegation under comitology change over time? Which shifts of power drove and ensued from these changes?' In this concluding chapter we (i) summarize our theoretical argument and empirical findings and (ii) develop some considerations about the future of delegation and comitology.

Our *theoretical approach* differs from the existing principal–agent literature, which focuses on why principals delegate in the first place and how principals seek to control the agents. Our main focus rests on the power distribution among the actors involved, the Council, the Commission, and the Parliament, linked to a change of institutional rule. To this end we base our argument on institutionalist bargaining theory and contend that all actors—in order to maximize their influence over policy outcomes—seek to obtain a mode of decision making that maximizes their institutional power.

Those losing out under an extant institutional rule will want to obtain more power and—by seeking to change the rules—they will gain more influence over policy outcomes. More specifically, if dissatisfied with a formal distribution of competences, the losers will seek to re-bargain these rules during their application. Since institutional rules are mostly incomplete contracts, they are subject to re-definition and re-bargaining in the course of their application. We analyse the conditions and processes of changing rules of delegation under comitology and account for why the Commission, the Council, and increasingly the Parliament did or did not choose to delegate decision making to the implementing powers of the Commission under comitology.

If comitology were chosen, we explain why specific rules governing the application of comitology, each implying more or less empowerment for the respective actors, were chosen. We particularly focus on the rising power of the Parliament under delegation and explain why the role of the Parliament in the governance of comitology has changed over time. We find that the Council and the Commission more frequently delegated implementing powers to the Commission as the legislative competences of the EP increased. It appears that the obligation to share legislative power with the Parliament motivates both the Council and the Commission to try to circumvent the Parliament through delegation, i.e. they seek to use comitology as an arena for the adoption of secondary legislation. In consequence, we expected that the Parliament would react to these attempts by opposing the use of delegation or restricting its use, and by seeking to increase its role under delegation. The first expectation was disconfirmed, the second and the third clearly confirmed.

We further discuss the principal–agent argument according to which delegation rules may be changed for efficiency-enhancing reasons in order to reduce transaction costs by delegating to comitology. Assuming an efficiency orientation of actors, we would have expected that the Council, following the empowerment of the Commission under the Comitology Decision of 1999, in order to 'get things done', would continue to favour delegation over legislation and we found some confirmation for this: with the changed Comitology Decision empowering the Commission, the Council still chose to delegate. Or to give another example: with co-decision and an additional principal (the Parliament), the Commission and the Council tend to delegate more. Our results give some support to this expectation; the Parliament does not oppose delegation, but systematically restricts its scope. This sheds light on the possible trade-off between the wish to maximize institutional power and the wish to find the best policy solution. Actors insisting on maximizing their institutional power may come to unsatisfactory policy solutions; and actors with only the best policy solution in mind may lose in institutional power.

By contrast our empirical accounts, both qualitative and quantitative, bear little evidence to support a sociological institutionalist argument claiming that the influence of democratic norms inevitably brought about the co-equal position of the Parliament in Delegated Acts under the Lisbon Treaty. Quite the opposite: the Parliament had to fight 'tooth and nail', pressuring, holding substantive decisions hostage across arenas, in order to bring about a change of institutional rules.

Hence, our rational institutionalist theoretical explanation can muster considerable empirical evidence of why in the long-term development of the delegation system the Parliament clearly emerges as winner. Both the Council and the Commission were willing to yield power to the Parliament in order to preserve the efficiency of the legislative and delegation process. The Parliament underlined its demands for a formal role in the delegation process by blocking decisions in the areas of legislation under co-decision and the budgetary process until—under the Lisbon Treaty—it obtained an almost co-equal role with the Council under delegation. These institutional changes in the delegation system of the European Union may easily be grasped by using an institutionalist power-based distributive bargaining explanation; but they also point to a need to focus on functional efficiency arguments in order to understand why member states in the Council and the Commission yielded to cross-arena pressure of the Parliament when granting it more competences.

In the qualitative empirical chapter we investigated the patterns and causes of the changes of comitology rules over time, focusing specifically on the rules defining the role that the Parliament played and plays under delegation. Assuming rules to be incomplete contracts, and taking as given multiple decision-making arenas and distinguishing between rule-designing actors in (rule-designing) arenas from substantive legislative decision makers deciding in (substantive) policy arenas, we argued that actors with no formal say in designing institutional rules can, by withholding their support for a decision in the substantive arena, indirectly influence institutional decisions taken in the rule-designing arena. Applied to the Parliament, we showed that indeed, our cross-arena linkage hypothesis is empirically confirmed.

The Parliament very successfully leveraged its bargaining power by threatening to withhold its support for a substantive legislative matter in the co-decision and/or budgetary arenas in order to exert indirect influence on the shaping of comitology rules. We contend that this has been the main driver of change in the comitology rules, and that it has resulted in a substantial increase of the Parliament's influence in delegation. Co-decision played an eminent role in offering the Parliament such an instrument for blocking the decision-making process not only in the legislative arena proper, but also in the institutional rule-designing arena. The Parliament also exploited the formal rules as far as possible by renegotiating them and modifying them endogenously in their daily application to its own advantage by taking certain issues 'hostage' in other linked arenas.

In the quantitative empirical chapters, we first offer a quantitative view of all legislative acts in order to situate delegation to comitology in the overall context of legislative activity, describing the broad patterns and trends in legislation and in the choice of instrument and the decision to delegate, in order to provide a background for the subsequent detailed analyses. What we found was a clear aggregate trend towards a higher share of Delegated Acts in each and every policy area. The analysis also provides evidence of a strong connection between the use of the most supranational legal instrument, i.e. regulations, and the use of delegated legislation across policy areas. We may therefore conclude that a common underlying logic of intergovernmentalism versus supranationalism is at work in the legislative process, which manifests itself similarly with respect to the choice of instrument and of delegation or non-delegation. We also find an increasing use of delegation since the introduction of co-decision, where Parliament became a co-equal legislator supporting our general hypothesis that—with empowerment of the Parliament—the Commission and the Council sought to circumvent the Parliament.

Proceeding to a sectoral quantitative statistical analysis, we first showed, for the area of environmental policy, that the Commission and the Council have indeed been more willing to rely on extensive delegation since the introduction of co-decision. The increase in delegation in the two years following the signing of the Amsterdam Treaty indicates that the Commission and the Council anticipated a relative loss of power to the Parliament, and rushed to delegate as much as possible to the Commission before the co-decision procedure took effect.

However, the Council was only willing to delegate more to the Commission on the condition that it could exert as much control as possible over the procedure by using regulatory committees—a condition that the Commission strategically anticipated in its delegation proposals. We also hypothesized that, with the introduction of co-decision, the Parliament would oppose delegation altogether. However, contrary to our expectations, we found that the Parliament did not oppose delegation as such, but instead systematically restricted its scope. This strategy allows the Parliament—without obstructing the efficiency of delegated decision making—to maintain as much power and influence as possible.

When the Council originally delegated implementing powers to the Commission to flesh out the details of legislation, it was on the proviso that the Commission should cooperate with member states in the co-mitology committees. Each of the various comitology procedures entailed a different distribution of competences between member states and the Commission. In a further statistical analysis of delegation items in agricultural policy between 1995 and 2003, we show that, after being empowered by the Second Comitology Decision of 1999, the Commission was more willing to rely on extensive delegation, relying particularly on management and regulatory procedures. But we also found, against our expectations, that—in spite of a relative loss of power due to a reform of comitology procedures—the Council did not oppose delegation after 1999 to any considerable extent, which may be explained by the fact that the Council would have had to have had unanimous approval in order to change the Commission's proposal.

Bearing in mind the extensive changes to which the delegation system was subject in its development up to the time of the Lisbon Treaty where the Parliament became a co-equal partner under Delegated Acts (Art. 290), the question arises: what has remained of the 'old' comitology system as we knew it?

Is comitology 'as we knew it' dead?

Our answer is, not just yet. When considering the practical necessities of Arts 290 and 291 TFEU, this answer appears quite self-evident. What kind of cooperation between the Commission and member states will emerge in place of the old comitology system under Delegated Acts (Art. 290 TFEU)? The Commission will have to work with consultative committees consisting of representatives of member state governments with an advisory function but no blocking power. If one envisages how the Council will prepare for a possible rejection of a Commission decision under Art. 290 TFEU, one can easily imagine that the Council would have to come up with something similar to a comitology system, i.e. committees of national representatives and/or experts responsible for specific regulatory issues.

Hence, since Art. 290 TFEU essentially gives the Council power of veto, it may well be that—while comitology 'as we know it' does not exist any longer under delegation—it will reinvent itself as a function of the need for expertise that member governments will offer the Commission when drafting decisions. In short, a modified comitology or advisory group system seems likely to emerge in the application of Art. 290 TFEU.

Since the Parliament under Art. 290 TFEU now has co-equal power to reject decisions and object to decisions of the Commission, the same practical questions of how to prepare for these ex post control functions emerge for the Parliament. It will thus have to make corresponding substantive preparations, cooperate in working groups, very likely in cooperation with the Commission and member state experts. Again, this may give rise to a new modified form of comitology that includes the Parliament. The beginnings of such a process in the application of Delegated Acts are emerging at the time of writing. The Commission invites experts from both the Council and the Parliament to participate in the drafting of decisions at an early, even pre-draft, stage (interview, EP, January 2012). In all expert groups the Commission now invites as a matter of course permanent representatives from twenty-seven member states and representatives of the Parliament.

Finally, the practical question arises of how the Council and the Parliament will coordinate their actions when one or both consider rejecting or objecting to a Commission decision under Art. 290 TFEU. Formally, either the Council or the Parliament could reject a Commission decision under Art. 290 TFEU. Therefore, there is no immediate need for coordination in order to obtain a rejection or objection. For practical policy reasons, however, it would be equally important for both the Council and the Parliament to know whether the other institution intends to proceed with a rejection or an objection. Some form of coordination in preparing the corresponding decisions will therefore have to develop. Since decisions in a setting of delegation will require specialized expertise, some form of trilogue involving Council, Parliament, and Commission representatives is likely to emerge in order to discuss substantive issues. This is another reason why new forms of comitology committees may be formed, this time including the Parliament.

With regard to implementing acts, we have seen above that in 2010 and 2011 they constituted the overwhelming majority of Commission implementing decisions. Hence, quantitatively, almost everything is still about 'comitology' in the classic sense (Art. 291 TFEU). The Council arguably tries to avoid Delegated Acts and to use implementing acts, if at all possible, because member states have stronger ex-ante rights in shaping Commission decision drafts. Moreover, if the phase of cooperation and coordination works well, there is no reason to invoke the formal rules of control at the stage of formal decision making. The role of the Parliament (Art. 291 TFEU), by contrast, is weaker than before under scrutinized regulatory procedure. The enhanced logic, that the control exercised by committees is the 'control of Member states', constitutes an objection against the demand that the Parliament or indeed the Council (being the two arms of the EU legislator) should have a role within committees. At the same time, this means no real loss for members of the Council since they reappear in the shape of 'member states'.

From an overall distribution of power perspective, in the Lisbon Treaty the notion of a clearer division of powers *à la Montesquieu* was served by the article on the Delegated Acts (Art. 290 TFEU). Art. 290 TFEU describes the Parliament and the Council as the legislator and the Commission as the executive power, giving the legislator the right of revocation and objection to the executive's decisions. Delegated Acts (Art. 290 TFEU) are a matter of horizontal delegation from the legislator to the executive. Implementing acts (Art. 291 TFEU), where the Commission is to be 'a master of technicalities', are a matter of vertical delegation from member states to the Commission.

As we have seen, the horizontal dimension of delegation so far—for reasons of lack of rule specification, but also the principal unwillingness of the Council to delegate—does not carry much weight. The fact was that the ambiguity of the provisions of Lisbon in Arts 290 and 291 TFEU triggered new rounds of renegotiation to specify details of the incomplete contracts. Even more, a new informal rule emerged as a compromise from a deadlock situation in which the Council, Parliament, and the Commission could not agree whether to use delegated or implementing acts. This lends a latest empirical illustration to our general claim of continuous institutional change of institutional rules as incomplete contracts.

The data: Sources and classification

In what follows, we will discuss the data sources and decisions made with respect to classification. We used the EUR-Lex (former CELEX) database to obtain the data. EUR-Lex is the most comprehensive source of legislative events in the EU. The system of categorization makes it easy to distinguish between the legal instruments as well as the date on which the legal acts were adopted.[1] However, identifying the policy area of each piece of legislation is more of a challenge.

Classification by policy area: Treaty articles and directory codes

It is of course necessary to define precisely what we mean by 'policy area'. While defining this in abstract terms may be easy, finding a suitable operational equivalent is not. The choices are strongly constrained by the available data-source. One obvious possibility is to determine the areas according to policy areas defined by the EEC/EC/EU Treaties. The treaties are organized into different parts, each subdivided into specific titles and chapters, with subject headings indicating substantive areas. For instance, part II, title II, in the original Treaty of Rome was entitled 'agriculture' and it encompassed Treaty Articles 40–47 EEC.[2]

We could therefore classify all legislative acts that cite Article 43 of the Treaty of Rome as belonging to the area of agriculture. One potential problem, of course, is that legal acts frequently cite more than one treaty article, and often the articles do not appear in the same chapter. This implies that we have to choose between counting acts more than once or, alternatively, selecting one policy field that we consider to be the primary one for any given act. The latter is not only problematic for conceptual reasons but also for practical ones related to the number of acts. If we were to rely on the legal base for classification into policy fields, Delegated Acts would be classified as belonging to the treaty chapter of the articles cited by the legal acts on which they are based. For practical reasons, such an approach is not feasible.

---

[1] The field 'date of document' was used to categorize the legal acts in time since this reflects the time of adoption.

[2] As amended at Lisbon, Title III is now called 'Agriculture and Fisheries', and the pertinent provisions are contained in Articles 38–44 of the Treaty on the Functioning of the European Union.

The most accurate source of information on legislative events, the Celex/EUR-Lex database,[3] employs a classification system for legal acts that does not allow us to directly identify the 'ultimate' treaty base of Delegated Acts. That is, the Delegated Acts are entered with information concerning their immediate legal base in secondary legislation only. No information is provided for the treaty articles on which the corresponding secondary legislation is based. To accurately capture the number of legislated and Delegated Acts based on specific treaty articles, we would have to search first for all the legislated acts and then go looking for each of the Delegated Acts that refer to those as their legal base—a formidable task, indeed, considering the amount of legislation.

We therefore decided to choose another method based on the classification system used in the Celex/EUR-Lex database. All legal acts are classified in specific directory codes that indicate a specific area of action such as competition, agriculture, or taxation. There is a clear relationship between the titles and chapters of the treaties and the names of the directory codes, but it is not a one-to-one relationship. For instance, there is a directory code for 'fisheries', but no specific title or chapter in any of the treaties with that precise subject heading. Indeed, prior to the amendments made by the Treaty of Lisbon, there was just the title of 'Agriculture', which referred to the two directory codes of agriculture and fisheries.[4] Compared to other classification tools that indicate the area of the legislation, such as the 'subject' entry, which have been applied inconsistently with respect to legal acts over time, the directory codes are a more reliable and easy source of information for identifying the policy field of acts.

The directory codes are as follows:

General, financial, and institutional matters
Customs union and free movement of goods
Agriculture
Fisheries
Freedom of movement for workers and social policy
Right of establishment and freedom to provide services
Transport policy
Competition policy
Taxation
Economic and monetary policy
External relations
Energy
Industrial policy and internal market
Regional policy and coordination of structural instruments
Environment, consumers, and health protection
Science, information, education, and culture

---

[3] In Koenig, Luetgern, and Danwoll's work on sources of information for EU legislation, they argue that CELEX (now EUR-Lex) is the most accurate database on EU legislative events, whereas PreLex has advantages when it comes to the legislative process (König et al. 2006).

[4] Lisbon appears to have addressed this anomaly. See note 2 above.

Law related to undertakings
Common, foreign, and security policy
Area of freedom, security, and justice
People's Europe

Before moving on to the description itself, it is necessary to analyse the content of the directory codes. It would have been risky to assume a fixed relationship between the codes given to the acts, the policy areas indicated by their names, and the seemingly equivalent titles and chapters of the treaties. Rather, the precise nature of the content must be closely examined to make sure that faulty conclusions concerning legislative patterns and trends are not drawn on the basis of this mode of presenting the data. Of course, we cannot evaluate the 'common denominator' of the acts categorized in the directory codes in substantive terms. But we can trace the relationship between the categories and the treaty base of the legislated acts found in them. As mentioned above, it would have required a heroic effort to identify the ultimate basis of Delegated Acts, and we therefore had to assume that such acts were classified in the same directory codes as the acts that provide them with a treaty base. This is a very plausible assumption which allows us to analyse the relationship between legislation and delegation for regulations and directives in different areas.

The actual content of the directory codes will be examined via two different routes. First, it will be examined how regulations and directives with a specific legal base are classified. That is, to what extent can we expect that acts citing specific treaty articles as their legal bases are classified in a given directory code? Or put differently, how concentrated are acts that cite a given treaty article to be found in a specific category? Secondly, we engage in the reverse question and ask: Which are the most frequent legal bases cited by acts in each of the directory codes? This may seem circular, but since there are huge differences in the number of acts that are based on different treaty articles it is important to consider both perspectives. A specific directory code may serve as a completely insignificant destination category for acts based on a specific treaty article, but it may still be the dominant basis for acts found in the directory code.

There are different possible causes of non-correspondence between treaty articles and directory codes. As mentioned previously in this section, legal acts often regulate activity that relates to more than one policy area. Social reality is not neatly compartmentalized according to abstract concepts, and regulation will consequently often cut across predefined policy fields. One consequence is that, as already discussed, many regulations and directives have multiple legal bases. Another is that the same laws are often classified in more than one directory code. Therefore, the number of laws found by adding up the number identified by searching each possible legal base clearly exceeds the total number of laws passed. Likewise, we find a higher number of laws if we add together the number of acts classified in each directory code than we do when we take the total number of laws classified in any of them. For instance, there are 336 regulations or directives that cite Article 235 of the Treaty of Rome as a legal base. But if we add up the number of regulations and directives that have this legal base in each directory code, we arrive at the number 400.

Those who label legal acts are likely to allocate categories based on an interpretation of the substantive content of the legal act rather than simply looking at the treaty articles cited. For instance, not all legal acts that cite Articles 43 (Rome/Maastricht) and 37 (Amsterdam/Nice), each of which is listed under the title of 'agriculture', are found in the directory code 'agriculture'. Hence, a procedure that defines the primary policy field of a specific act and classifies it accordingly offers a more accurate picture of the amount of regulation in different areas. However, as with any act of interpretation, the method may be criticized for inconsistency in the criteria used. Similar acts may be classified in just one or in several directory codes, depending on the person labelling the acts.

To sum up, the lack of direct correspondence between legal base and directory code can be explained by the fact that overlap between policy areas is likely to give rise to the use of multiple legal bases, but when acts are classified in the directory codes, an interpretation of what the main substantive content is underlies the decision to classify the acts in just one or a few directory codes. Moreover, it cannot be ruled out that misclassification is an additional source of non-correspondence between treaty articles and directory codes.

From legal bases of acts to directory code
The first step of examining the relationship between directory codes and treaty articles is tracing the destination categories of directives/regulations based in the individual treaty articles. Searches were made for parts I–III of the Treaties of Rome and Maastricht (I. Principles; II. Foundations of the Community; III. Policy of the Community); and Amsterdam and Nice (I. Principles; II. Citizenship of the Union; III. Community Policies). These parts of the treaties were the ones most relevant to substantive policymaking in the European Community. Only treaty articles that give rise to more than two regulations or directives are regarded as

Table A1.1 Destination categories of directives/regulations based in the individual treaty articles

	The Community Treaties (1)			
	TEEC	TEC	TEC	TEC
	Original	Maastricht	Amsterdam	Nice
Number of 'active' treaty articles	35	24	23	28
100%	15	10	14	9
	(43%)	(42%)	(61%)	(32%)
> 90%	22	14	16	14
	(63%)	(58%)	(70%)	(50%)
> 80%	26	18	17	16
	(74%)	(75%)	(74%)	(57%)
> 70%	30	21	20	18
	(86%)	(87.5%)	(87%)	(64%)
< 50%	2	0	0	0
	(6%)	(0%)	(0%)	(0%)

'active' and were included in the table (see Table A1.1). Moreover, only the two to three main recipient directory codes were considered.

A summary of the results are presented in Table A1.1.

As can be seen from Table A1.1, thirty-five treaty articles in the relevant parts of the Original Treaty of Rome, including the Single European Act (SEA) gave rise to more than two regulations or directives. Fifteen of these (i.e. 43 per cent) had all their derived acts classified in one specific directory code, while twenty-two had over 90 per cent of the acts based on them in one category, twenty-six had over 80 per cent in one category. Finally, thirty acts had over 70 per cent of the acts based on them in one category. A similar pattern of correspondence between treaty articles and directory codes may be observed in the analysis of classification practices for the other three treaties. We thus find that over 80 per cent of the regulations/directives that cite a specific treaty article are found in one particular directory code in seventy-five of the cases—although it is slightly fewer (57 per cent) for acts adopted under the Nice Treaty. It is also notable that very few treaty articles—and only under the Treaty of Rome, where it was two articles (or 6 per cent of the total)—give rise to acts of which less than half are found in the dominant category.

There is thus evidence of a reasonably high correspondence between treaty articles and directory codes.

However, in order to measure the extent of this correspondence, it is necessary to look not only at the relationship between treaty article and directory code, but also to consider what part the quantity of legislation plays in the relationship. If the high correspondence between treaty articles and dominant directory codes is caused by those articles that give rise to relatively few acts, the correspondence may be less in quantitative terms. As a measure of concentration of treaty articles in directory codes, the following method was used. The share of acts that cite a particular legal base as a proportion of the total number of acts adopted for this treaty was multiplied by the percentage of these acts that can be found in the dominant directory code. Let TAi signify the number of regulations and directives citing a particular treaty article i, $TAall$ the total number of regulations and directives citing any of the treaty articles examined, and $DCpct$ the highest percentage of TAi found in one single directory code. The formula for the treaty article directory code correspondence (TADC) can thus be written:

$$TADC = \sum \left(\frac{TA_i}{TA_{all}} \right) \times DC_{pct}$$

The TADC gives an overall measure of correspondence or concentration of acts citing a particular treaty article in a single directory code. If all acts citing a particular legal base were always found in one particular directory code (which does not preclude the same act from also appearing in other directory codes), TADC would equal 100. On the other hand, given that the number of directory codes is 20, the lowest score possible is 5. This would signify a situation where acts citing a given treaty article are found equally in all directory codes. The summary scores were as follows in Table A1.2.

Table A1.2 Treaty article directory code correspondence

	The Community Treaties (2)			
	TEEC	TEC	TEC	TEC
	(Original & SEA)	(Maastricht)	(Amsterdam)	(Nice)
TADC	74.4	73.7	77.7	73.2

As can be seen, the scores are very similar across the four treaty periods and are relatively high. That is, they show us that on average we can expect to find some 75 per cent of the acts citing a particular legal base classified in one particular directory code. Considering the points discussed above related to the use of multiple legal bases and classification principles based on the main themes of the legal acts, this can be regarded as very high. Moreover, the correspondence between single treaty articles and their dominant destination categories are investigated here, but if we had included the investigation to measure percentage in the top two categories, it is clear that even higher concentration scores would be observed. However, it does not tell us how many other categories are also used.

From directory code to legal base of acts

The second step is analysis of the content in each directory code. That is, when we search for directives and regulations in particular directory codes, what do we find? This is important in order to be able to interpret quantitative trends related to the individual categories.

In this section we describe the most frequently cited legal bases of the regulations and directives found in individual directory codes. Due to the relatively low number of such acts categorized in them and/or due to a high spread in the legal bases cited by these acts, some will not be included in the subsequent analysis and quantitative description of policy areas. These omitted directory codes are: 1. General, financial, and institutional matters; 10. Economic and monetary policy and free movement of capital; 12. Energy; 14. Regional policy and coordination of structural instruments; 16. Science, information, education, and culture; 17. Law relating to undertakings; 18. Common, foreign, and security policy; 19. Area of freedom, security, and justice; 20. People's Europe. Moreover, only sub-division 5.2., Social Policy, was described for directory code 5: Freedom of movement for workers and social policy.

The detailed tables describing the content of the directory codes are in Appendix 2, while a shorter summary is presented in Table A1.3. The treaty articles are given the prefix 'r' or 'a', which indicates whether the article follows the numbering of the orginal Treaty of Rome or the Treaty of Amsterdam. For example, r43 means Article 43 of the Treaty of Rome, i.e. Article 43 TEEC/TEC [Original & SEA; Maastricht]); a133 means Article 133 TEC (Amsterdam, Nice). Finally, also included is the category of 'overlap', where the extent of overlap with other directory codes is mentioned. It gives us an indication of the extent to which acts in one directory code are also classified in others. Only overlaps of over 5 per cent of the total number of acts in the directory code described will be mentioned in the table.

Table A1.3 Content of the directory codes (summary)

Directory Code	Dominant Legal Bases	Main differences in legal bases cited across periods	Overlap	Similarity in legal base
Customs Union and Free Movement of Goods	r28/a26 and r113/a133 on common customs tariff and common commercial policy. 93–97% of all acts found cite one of these.	Article r43 is cited to a significant extent (12%) in the period until TEC Maastricht, but only then.	11% of acts in agriculture. 10% of acts in external relations.	Very high
Agriculture	r43/a37 concern agriculture. 71–85% of acts cite this. The article r113/a133 on common customs tariff and commercial policy is cited by 10–15%. These articles together are cited by 81–96% of the acts.	The article r113/a133 is cited 10–15% until the TEC Nice. After the TEC Amsterdam came into force, 10–15% cited the public health article a152. 96% of acts cite one of these in the period before the TEC Amsterdam, and 81–86% after.	11% of its acts are also classified in external relations. 3% are also in customs union.	Very high
Fisheries	r43/a37 on agriculture. Cited by 88–98% of the acts. Article r113/a133 on the common commercial policy is cited second most, followed by a152 on public health. The two dominant treaty articles account for a very high 93–98% of the total number of acts classified in this code.	r113/a133 is cited 13% and 5% in the periods under TEEC (Original) and TEC Amsterdam, but not otherwise. Under TEC Nice only, the article a152 on public health is cited by 8%.	7% of acts are also in external relations. 1% is also in agriculture.	Very high
Social Policy	r51 concerning social security and worker mobility and a137 on social provisions. Together cited by 17–38% across periods. r235/a308 concerning attainment of community objectives cited by 25–36% of the acts. Articles on discrimination, cooperation in the social field, implementation of the	r2, r7, and r127 cited only before TEC Maastricht entered into force. a139 cited under TEC Amsterdam only and a42 + a308 cited only after TEC Nice entered into force.	6% also in agriculture, 6% in transport, and 5% in environment, consumers, and health protection	Low. Dispersed legal base.

	cited. The three most dominant articles do not account for more than 50–67% of the total number of acts.		
Right of Establishment and Freedom to Provide Services	r57/a47 on professional qualifications and mutual recognition thereof is cited by 55–77% of acts in this code across periods. r66/a55 on freedom to provide services is cited by 32–38% of the acts. r100/a95 on approximation of laws for common market is cited by 21–32%. The two dominant articles do not cover more than 63–74% of the acts.	54r on abolishing restrictions to free establishment cited only before TEC Maastricht entered into force. r75/a80 on transport cited only in periods under TECs Maastricht and Nice.	9% also classified in transport and 8% in industrial policy and internal market.	Medium to high
Transport	r75/a71 and r84/a80 articles on transport are cited by 81–90% of the acts in this category.	r87 on competition rules for undertakings and r100 on approximation of laws are cited by 15% under TEEC but not under later treaties.	15% of acts also in industrial policy and internal market. 7% are shared with environment, consumers, and health protection; and 6% in competition	
Competition	Few legislated acts in this category. Articles from the chapter on competition policy are cited (r85–r94/a81–a89). The two dominant acts here account for 50–88% of the acts found.	r113 on the common commercial policy is cited by 25–39% under TEEC and TEC Maastricht only. r75 on transport is only cited by 15% under TEC Maastricht	25% of its acts also in transport and 17% shared with industrial policy and the internal market.	High
Taxation	Few acts in this category. r99/a93 concerning the harmonization of indirect taxation is cited by 72–95% of acts in all treaty periods except for Amsterdam, where a96 on competition distortion is cited by 87%. r100/a94 on approximation of laws is cited by 28–60%.	r99/a93 is cited most in all periods except under TEC Amsterdam, where it is not cited. a96 on competition distortion is only an important base under TEC Amsterdam.	Does not overlap to any significant extent with other codes	Very High

Continued

Table A1.3 *Continued*

Directory Code	Dominant Legal Bases	Main differences in legal bases cited across periods	Overlap	Similarity in legal base
External Relations	85–100% of acts cite one of the two prominent treaty articles. r113/a133 on common commercial policy is cited by 50–80% and r43/a37 on agriculture is cited by 16–22% of the acts across the periods. The two most cited articles are mentioned by 68–90% of acts.	Under the TEC Maastricht, article a228 on international agreements is cited frequently, but under TECs Amsterdam and Nice articles of development cooperation (a179) and the cooperation with third countries (a181) makes up a smaller share of 6–13%.	36% also in agriculture – and 8% with customs union	High
Industrial Policy and Internal Market	r100/a95 on approximation of laws for common market is cited by 54–84% of acts in the four treaty periods. r43/a37 on agriculture is cited by 6–16% of the acts.	On public health and environment cited by 5–10% under TECs Amsterdam and Nice.	15% of the acts also in environment, consumers, and health protection, 10% with external relations, and 9% in agriculture, respectively.	High
Environment, Consumers, and Health Protection	r100/a95 on approximation of laws for common market is cited by 34–60% across periods, and r130s/a175 on the environment by 18–38%. In addition, other articles such as r43/a37 on agricultural policy and a152 on public health are also cited, but to a minor extent. The two most frequently cited articles account for a relatively high 68–78% of acts in the code across the four treaty periods.	a152 on public health cited by 19 and 8% under TECs Amsterdam and Nice, but not others.	26% also in agriculture, 20% in industrial policy and internal market, and 8% also in external relations.	Moderately high

Directory codes

Table A2.1 Directory Code 2: Customs Union and Free Movement of Goods

Treaty	Articles	Number	%age	Subject matter
TEEC Original &		**2413**		
SEA	28	1683	70%	alteration/suspension of common customs tariff
	113	623	26%	common commercial policy
	43	288	12%	common agricultural policy
	28 or 113	2247	93%	
TEC Maastrict		**236**		
	28	80	34%	alteration/suspension of common customs tariff
	113	159	67%	common commercial policy
	28 or 113	230	97%	
TEC Amsterdam		**88**		
	26	34	39%	fixing common tariff duties
	133	50	57%	common commercial policy
	26 or 133	82	93%	
TEC Nice		**54**		
	26	23	43%	fixing common tariff duties
	133	28	52%	common commercial policy
	26 or 133	50	93%	

Table A2.2 Directory Code 3: Agriculture

Treaty	Articles	Number	%age	Subject matter
TEEC Original &		**1750**		
SEA	42	184	11%	competition and aid to agriculture
	43	1483	85%	common agricultural policy
	100	119	7%	approximation of laws (common market)
	113	257	15%	common commercial policy
	43 or 113	1681	96%	
TEC Maastrict		**291**		
	42	57	20%	competition and aid to agriculture
	43	226	78%	common agricultural policy
	113	54	19%	common commercial policy
	43 or 113	278	96%	
TEC Amsterdam		**125**		
	37	94	75%	common agricultural policy
	133	15	12%	common commercial policy
	152	14	11%	public health
	37 or 133	107	86%	
TEC Nice		**98**		
	37	70	71%	common agricultural policy
	152	15	15%	public health
	37 or 152	79	81%	

Table A2.3 Directory Code 4: Fisheries

Treaty	Articles	Number	%age	Subject matter
TEEC Original &		**188**		
SEA	42	22	12%	competition and aid to agriculture
	43	165	88%	common agricultural policy
	103	10	5%	approximation of laws (common market)
	113	24	13%	common commercial policy
	43 or 113	174	93%	
TEC Maastrict		**98**		
	43	96	98%	competition and aid to agriculture
TEC Amsterdam		**58**		
	37	54	93%	common agricultural policy
	133	3		common commercial policy
	37 or 133	57	98%	
TEC Nice		**64**		
	37	58	91%	common agricultural policy
	152	5	8%	public health
	37 or 152	63	98%	

Table A2.4 Directory Code 5.2: Social Policy

Treaty	Articles	Number	% age	Subject matter
TEEC Original		**117**		
& SEA	2	13	11%	goal of common market
	7	13	11%	against discrimination of nationalities
	51	28	24%	social security to ensure worker mobility
	100	18	15%	approximation of laws for common market
	118	21	18%	cooperation in social field
	127	7	6%	implementation of social fund
	235	29	25%	attaining community objectives not empowered
	51 or 118 or 235	63	54%	
TEC Maastrict		**36**		
	51	9	25%	social security to ensure worker mobility
	100	7	19%	approximation of laws for common market
	118	7	19%	cooperation in social field
	235	13	36%	attain community objectives
	51 or 118 or 235	20	56%	
TEC Amsterdam		**21**		
	137	8	38%	social provisions
	139	3	14%	agreements of management and labour
	283	3	14%	staff regulations in EC
	137 or 139 or 283	14	67%	
TEC Nice		**36**		
	42	5	14%	common agricultural policy
	137	6	17%	social provisions
	308	12	33%	attain community objectives
	42 or 137 or 108	18	50%	

Table A2.5 Directory Code 6: Right of Establishment and Freedom to Provide Services

Treaty	Articles	Number	%age	Subject matter
TEEC Original &		**112**		
SEA	49	30	27%	free movement of workers
	54	18	16%	abolish restrictions of free establishment
	57	70	63%	professional qualifications (recognitition)
	66	43	38%	freedom to provide services
	100	23	21%	approximation of laws (common market)
	57 or 66	70	63%	
TEC Maastrict		**34**		
	49	4	12%	free movement of workers
	57	21	62%	professional qualifications (recognitition)
	66	12	35%	freedom to provide services
	75	5	15%	rules for transport
	100	11	32%	approximation of laws (common market)
	57 or 66	25	74%	
TEC Amsterdam		**26**		
	40	3	12%	free movement of workers
	47	20	77%	professional qualifications (recognition)
	55	10	38%	freedom to provide services
	95	7	27%	approximation of laws (common market)
	47 or 55	20	77%	
TEC Nice		**22**		
	47	12	55%	professional qualifications (recognition)
	55	7	32%	freedom to provide services
	80	3	14%	transport (types covered)
	95	7	32%	approximation of laws (common market)
	47 or 55 or 95	15	68%	

Table A2.6 Directory Code 7: Transport Policy

Treaty	Articles	Number	%age	Subject matter
TEEC Original &		**184**		
SEA	75	117	64%	rules of transport
	84	33	18%	transport (types covered)
	87	9	5%	competition rules for undertakings
	100	18	10%	approximation of laws (common market)
	75 or 84	149	81%	
TEC Maastrict		**51**		
	75	28	55%	rules for transport
	84	19	37%	transport (types covered)
	75 or 84	46	90%	
TEC Amsterdam		**38**		
	71	15	39%	rules for transport
	80	19	50%	transport (types covered)
	71 or 80	34	89%	
TEC Nice		**59**		
	71	18	31%	rules for transport
	80	36	61%	transport (types covered)
	71 or 80	52	88%	

Table A2.7 Directory Code 8: Competition Policy

Treaty	Articles	Number	%age	Subject matter
	87	17	47%	competition rules for undertakings
	90	5	14%	competition rules for public undertakings
	92	9	25%	competition rules for state aid
	113	9	25%	competition commercial policy
	75	3	17%	rules for transport
	90	4	22%	competition rules for public undertakings
	92	7	39%	competition rules for state aid
	94	7	39%	application of competition rules and exemption
	113	7	39%	common commercial policy
	92 or 94: 9	9	50%	
TEC		**8**		
Amsterdam	83	3	38%	competition rules for undertakings
	86	2	25%	competition rules for public undertakings
	83 or 86	5	63%	
TEC Nice		**6**		
	83	3	50%	competition rules for undertakings
	86	2	33%	competition rules for public undertakings
	83 or 86	52	88%	

Table A2.8 Directory Code 9: Taxation

Treaty	Articles	Number	%age	Subject matter
TEEC Original &		**78**		
SEA	99	74	95%	harmonization of indirect taxation
	100	47	60%	approximation of laws (common market)
	99 or 100	78	100%	
TEC Maastrict		**13**		
	99	11	85%	harmonization of indirect taxation
TEC Amsterdam		**15**		
	94	7	47%	approximation of laws (common market)
	96	13	87%	competition distortion
	94 or 96	13	87%	
TEC Nice		**25**		
	93	18	72%	harmonization of indirect taxation
	94	7	28%	approximation of laws (common market)
	93 or 94	25	100%	

Table A2.9 Directory Code 11: External Relations

Treaty	Articles	Number	%age	Subject matter
TEEC Original		**1077**		
& SEA	43	171	16%	common agricultural policy
	113	865	80%	common commercial policy
	43 or 113	985	91%	
TEC Maastrict		**281**		
	43	45	16%	common agricultural policy
	113	178	63%	common commercial policy
	130	20	7%	European investment bank (loan/ financing)
	228	63	22%	international agreements
	113 or 228	235	84%	
TEC Amsterdam		**141**		
	37	25	18%	common agricultural policy
	133	84	60%	common commercial policy
	179	9	6%	development cooperation
	37 or 133	108	77%	
TEC Nice		**139**		
	37	31	22%	common agricultural policy
	133	70	50%	common commercial policy
	179	11	8%	development cooperation
	181	18	13%	cooperation with third countries
	37 or 133	95	68%	

Table A2.10 Directory Code 13: Industrial Policy and Internal Market

Treaty	Articles	Number	% age	Subject matter
TEEC Original		**473**		
& SEA	43	44	9%	common agricultural policy
	75	16	3%	rules for transport
	100	396	84%	approximation of laws (common market)
	113	13	3%	common commercial policy
	43 or 100	410	87%	
TEC Maastrict		**110**		
	43	8	7%	common agricultural policy
	66	5	5%	freedom to provide services
	90	4	4%	competition rules for public undertakings
	94	5	5%	application of competition rules and exemptions
	100	78	71%	approximation of laws (common market)
	113	8	7%	common commercial policy
	100 or 113 or 43	90	82%	
TEC Amsterdam		**79**		
	37	13	16%	common agricultural policy
	47	8	10%	mutual recognition of qualifications
	55	5	6%	freedom to provide services
	95	43	54%	approximation of laws (common market)
	175	4	5%	environment
	37 or 95	56	71%	
TEC Nice		**93**		
	37	6	6%	common agricultural policy
	71	4	4%	approximation of laws (common market)
	95	62	67%	approximation of laws (common market)
	152	6	6%	public health
	175	6	6%	environment
	47 or 55 or 95	15	68%	

Table A2.11 Directory Code 15: Environment, Consumers, and Health Protection

Treaty	Articles	Number	%age	Subject matter
TEEC Original &		**206**		
SEA	43	15	7%	common agricultural policy
	100	124	60%	approximation of laws (common market)
	130s	38	18%	environment
	113	9	4%	common commercial policy
	100 or 130s	161	78%	
TEC Maastrict		**64**		
	43	7	11%	common agricultural policy
	84	3	5%	types of transport covered by policy
	100	22	34%	approximation of laws (common market)
	130s	24	38%	environment
	130w	5	8%	development cooperation
	100 or 130s	48	75%	
TEC Amsterdam		**70**		
	37	6	8%	agriculture
	80	4	5%	professional qualifications (recognition)
	95	27	34%	approximation of laws (common market)
	152	15	19%	public health
	175	27	34%	environment
	95 to 175	54	68%	
TEC Nice		**90**		
	37	11	12%	agriculture
	80	6	7%	professional qualification (recognition)
	95	36	40%	approximation of laws (common market)
	152	7	8%	public health
	175	29	32%	environment
	95 or 175	63	70%	

Number of laws adopted in policy areas per five years

Table A3.1 Customs Union and Free Movement of Goods

		1970–4	1975–9	1980–4	1985–9	1990–4	1995–9	2000–4	2005–6	All Years
Regulations	All	546	1133	1592	1591	1376	802	550	420	7731
	Legislated	325	507	617	676	380	161	95	72,5	2790
	Delegated	221	626	975	915	996	641	455	347,5	4941
Directives	All	8	21	18	5	3	2	4	5	62
	Legislated	2	8	5	2	3	2	3	5	26
	Delegated	6	13	13	3	0	0	1	0	36
% Regulations of total		99%	98%	99%	100%	100%	100%	99%	99%	99%
% Delegation	Regulations	40%	55%	61%	58%	72%	80%	83%	83%	64%
	Directives	75%	62%	72%	60%	0%	0%	25%	0%	58%
	Combined	41%	55%	61%	58%	72%	80%	82%	82%	64%

Table A3.2 Agriculture

		1970–4	1975–9	1980–4	1985–9	1990–4	1995–9	2000–4	2005–6	All Years
Regulations	All	636	1514	3097	4158	4154	3054	2000	2010	19427
	Legislated	90	273	410	447	305	192	112	112,5	1898
	Delegated	546	1241	2687	3711	3849	2895	1888	1897,5	17529
Directives	All	57	99	115	138	192	132	149	85	963
	Legislated	34	50	56	61	88	46	37	2,5	381
	Delegated	23	49	59	77	105	86	112	82,5	582
% Regulations		92%	94%	96%	97%	96%	96%	93%	96%	95%
% Delegated	Regulations	86%	82%	87%	89%	93%	95%	94%	94%	90%
	Directives	40%	49%	51%	56%	54%	65%	75%	97%	60%
	Combined	82%	80%	85%	88%	91%	94%	93%	95%	89%

Table A3.3 Fisheries

		1970–4	1975–9	1980–4	1985–9	1990–4	1995–9	2000–4	2005–6	All Years
Regulations	All	19	70	308	632	737	542	448	485	2942
	Legislated	3	32	57	44	66	88	76	77,5	407
	Delegated	16	38	251	588	671	454	371	405	2535
Directives	All	0	0	1	0	0	1	0	2,5	2
	Legislated	0	0	1	0	0	1	0	0	1
	Delegated	0	0	0	0	0	0	0	2,5	1
% Regulations		100%	100%	100%	100%	100%	100%	100%	99%	100%
% Delegated	Regulations	84%	54%	81%	93%	91%	84%	83%	84%	86%
	Directives			0%			0%		100%	50%
	Combined	84%	54%	81%	93%	91%	84%	83%	84%	86%

Table A3.4 Social Policy

		1970–4	1975–9	1980–4	1985–9	1990–4	1995–9	2000–4	2005–6	All Years
Regulations	All	11	18	25	23	17	18	18	55	164
	Legislated	10	15	16	13	13	14	22	27,5	108
	Delegated	1	3	9	10	4	4	16	27,5	56
Directives	All	4	8	9	12	29	23	26	17,5	110
	Legislated	4	7	9	12	27	19	25	12,5	101
	Delegated	0	1	0	0	2	4	1	5	9
% Regulations of total		73%	69%	74%	66%	37%	44%	41%	76%	60%
% Delegated	Regulations	9%	17%	36%	43%	24%	22%	89%	50%	34%
	Directives	0%	13%	0%	0%	7%	17%	4%	29%	8%
	Combined	7%	15%	26%	29%	13%	20%	39%	45%	24%

Table A3.5 Right of Establishment and Freedom to Provide Services

		1970–4	1975–9	1980–4	1985–9	1990–4	1995–9	2000–4	2005–6	All Years
Regulations	All	0	0	0	1	8	8	9	17,5	34
	Legislated	0	0	0	1	7	3	3	2,5	16
	Delegated	0	0	0	0	1	5	6	15	18
Directives	All	16	20	13	33	36	35	28	40	201
	Legislated	16	20	13	31	32	28	20	30	181
	Delegated	0	0	0	2	4	7	8	10	20
% Regulations		0%	0%	0%	3%	18%	19%	24%	30%	14%
% Delegated	Regulations				0%	13%	63%	67%	86%	53%
	Directives	0%	0%	0%	6%	11%	20%	29%	25%	10%
	Combined	0%	0%	0%	6%	11%	28%	38%	43%	16%

Table A3.6 Transport

		1970–4	1975–9	1980–4	1985–9	1990–4	1995–9	2000–4	2005–6	All Years
Regulations	All	19	22	11	30	59	35	64	100	278
	Legislated	15	20	9	21	37	15	34	25	162
	Delegated	4	2	2	9	22	20	30	75	116
Directives	All	2	15	17	21	39	54	61	55	231
	Legislated	2	15	17	20	37	33	34	35	174
	Delegated	0	0	0	1	2	21	27	20	57
% Regulations		90%	59%	39%	59%	60%	39%	51%	65%	55%
% Delegated	Regulations	21%	9%	18%	30%	37%	57%	47%	75%	42%
	Directives	0%	0%	0%	5%	5%	39%	44%	36%	25%
	Combined	19%	5%	7%	20%	24%	46%	46%	61%	34%

Table A3.7 Competition Policy

		1970–4	1975–9	1980–4	1985–9	1990–4	1995–9	2000–4	2005–6	All Years
Regulations	All	6	2	8	11	21	26	23	27,5	107
	Legislated	4	0	0	5	8	13	4	5	36
	Delegated	2	2	8	6	13	13	19	22,5	72
Directives	All	0	1	5	3	8	4	2	5	25
	Legislated	0	1	5	1	5	0	0	0	11
	Delegated	0	0	0	2	3	4	2	5	14
% Regulations of total		100%	67%	62%	79%	72%	87%	92%	85%	81%
D/L-Ratio	Regulations	33%	100%	100%	55%	62%	50%	83%	82%	67%
	Directives		0%	0%	67%	38%	100%	100%	100%	56%
	Combined	33%	67%	62%	57%	55%	57%	84%	85%	65%

Table A3.8 Taxation

		1970–4	1975–9	1980–4	1985–9	1990–4	1995–9	2000–4	2005–6	All Years
Regulations	All	0	1	1	0	7	7	7	12,5	28
	Legislated	0	0	0	0	1	3	4	0	8
	Delegated	0	1	1	0	6	4	3	12,5	20
Directives	All	9	16	19	19	21	12	23	25	129
	Legislated	9	15	19	17	20	12	23	20	123
	Delegated	0	1	0	2	1	0	0	5	6
% Regulations		0%	6%	5%	0%	25%	37%	23%	33%	18%
D/L-Ratio	Regulations		100%	100%		86%	57%	43%	100%	71%
	Directives	0%	6%	0%	11%	5%	0%	0%	20%	5%
	Combined	0%	12%	5%	11%	25%	21%	10%	47%	17%

Table A3.9 External Relations

		1970–4	1975–9	1980–4	1985–9	1990–4	1995–9	2000–4	2005–6	All Years
Regulations	All	107	391	1436	1374	1226	715	776	600	6262
	Legislated	101	195	346	223	288	214	186	155	1635
	Delegated	7	196	1090	1151	938	501	590	445	4627
Directives	All	4	1	1	0	0	1	2	0	9
	Legislated	4	1	1	0	0	1	2	0	9
	Delegated	0	0	0	0	0	0	0	0	0
% Regulations		96%	100%	100%	100%	100%	100%	100%	100%	100%
D/L-Ratio	Regulations	7%	50%	76%	84%	77%	70%	76%	74%	74%
	Directives	0%	0%	0%			0%	0%		0%
	Combined	6%	50%	76%	84%	77%	70%	76%	74%	74%

Table A3.10 Industrial Policy and Internal Market

		1970–4	1975–9	1980–4	1985–9	1990–4	1995–9	2000–4	2005–6	All Years
Regulations	All	1	19	132	6	29	47	72	122,5	354
	Legislated	1	8	15	3	14	19	33	35	107
	Delegated	0	11	117	3	15	28	39	87,5	247
Directives	All	75	138	132	163	198	189	199	190	1167
	Legislated	70	106	78	98	114	78	91	65	661
	Delegated	5	32	54	65	84	111	108	125	505
% Regulations		1%	12%	50%	4%	13%	20%	27%	39%	23%
% Delegated	Regulations	0%	58%	89%	50%	52%	60%	54%	71%	70%
	Directives	7%	23%	41%	40%	42%	59%	54%	66%	43%
	Combined	7%	27%	65%	40%	44%	59%	54%	68%	49%

Table A3.11 Environment, Consumers, and Health Protection

		1970–4	1975–9	1980–4	1985–9	1990–4	1995–9	2000–4	2005–6	All Years
Regulations	All	0	1	10	39	73	117	226	212,5	546
	Legislated	0	0	4	22	31	20	48	45	134
	Delegated	0	1	6	17	42	97	178	167,5	412
Directives	All	8	33	39	68	70	64	84	102,5	407
	Legislated	6	29	35	53	54	38	55	60	297
	Delegated	2	4	4	15	16	26	29	42,5	110
% Regulations		0%	3%	20%	36%	51%	65%	73%	67%	57%
% Delegated	Regulations		100%	60%	44%	58%	83%	79%	79%	75%
	Directives	25%	12%	10%	22%	23%	41%	35%	41%	27%
	Combined	25%	15%	20%	30%	41%	68%	67%	67%	55%

Average number of laws in force in policy area per five years

Table A4.1 DC: 02 Customs Union and Free Movement of Goods

		1970–4	1975–9	1980–4	1985–9	1990–4	1995–9	2000–4	2005–7
Regulations	All	113	596	187	298	395	452	576	667
	Legislated	17	45	14	29	31	60	41	50
	Delegated	96	551	173	269	364	393	535	618
Directives	All	3	15	21	17	8	5	5	4
	Legislated	1	5	5	3	1	1	2	2
	Delegated	2	11	16	14	6	4	3	2
% Regulations		97%	97%	90%	95%	98%	99%	99%	99%
% Delegation	Regulations	85%	92%	93%	90%	92%	87%	93%	93%
	Directives	53%	70%	76%	81%	82%	74%	64%	50%
	Combined	84%	92%	91%	90%	92%	87%	93%	92%

Table A4.2 DC: Agriculture

		1970–4	1975–9	1980–4	1985–9	1990–4	1995–9	2000–4	2005–7
Regulations	All	563	1207	2007	2712	3196	3024	3002	3620
	Legislated	240	487	747	875	800	368	218	207
	Delegated	323	720	1260	1837	2396	2656	2784	3413
Directives	All	49	128	222	251	268	224	238	328
	Legislated	38	84	135	173	162	80	71	72
	Delegated	11	44	87	78	106	144	167	256
% Regulations		92%	90%	90%	92%	92%	93%	93%	92%
% Delegation	Regulations	57%	60%	63%	68%	75%	88%	93%	94%
	Directives	22%	34%	39%	31%	40%	64%	70%	78%
	Combined	55%	57%	60%	65%	72%	86%	91%	93%

Table A4.3 DC: 04 Fisheries

		1970–4	1975–9	1980–4	1985–9	1990–4	1995–9	2000–4	2005–7
Regulations	All	628	648	668	718	781	802	794	1033
	Legislated	620	626	643	664	657	655	643	663
	Delegated	8	22	25	54	124	147	151	370
Directives	All	1	1	1	2	2	1	1	1
	Legislated	1	1	1	2	2	1	1	1
	Delegated	0	0	0	0	0	0	0	0
% Regulations		100%	100%	100%	100%	100%	100%	100%	100%
% Delegation	Regulationss	1%	3%	4%	7%	16%	18%	19%	36%
	Directives	0%	0%	0%	0%	0%	0%	0%	0%
	Combined	1%	3%	4%	7%	16%	18%	19%	36%

Table A4.4 DC: 05.2 Social Policy

		1970–4	1975–9	1980–4	1985–9	1990–4	1995–9	2000–4	2005–7
Regulations	All	25	35	33	36	30	21	26	50
	Legislated	25	33	32	32	24	16	12	21
	Delegated	1	2	1	4	6	5	13	29
Directives	All	4	13	20	26	28	15	13	10
	Legislated	4	13	19	25	26	11	11	7
	Delegated	0	0	1	1	2	4	2	4
% Regulations		86%	73%	63%	58%	52%	58%	66%	83%
% Delegation	Regulations	2%	6%	3%	10%	19%	25%	52%	59%
	Directives	0%	2%	5%	4%	6%	25%	15%	35%
	Combined	2%	5%	4%	8%	13%	25%	39%	55%

Table A4.5 DC: 06 Right of Establishment and Freedom to Provide Services

		1970–4	1975–9	1980–4	1985–9	1990–4	1995–9	2000–4	2005–7
Regulations	All	0	0	0	1	3	3	8	18
	Legislated	0	0	0	1	2	1	1	3
	Delegated	0	0	0	0	1	2	7	15
Directives	All	39	58	74	91	74	20	17	31
	Legislated	39	58	74	91	72	13	9	17
	Delegated	0	0	0	0	1	7	8	13
% Regulations		0%	0%	0%	1%	4%	13%	32%	37%
% Delegation	Regulations				0%	20%	73%	93%	85%
	Directives	0%	0%	0%	0%	2%	35%	47%	43%
	Combined				0%	3%	40%	62%	59%

Table A4.6 DC: 07 Transport

		1970–4	1975–9	1980–4	1985–9	1990–4	1995–9	2000–4	2005–7
Regulations	All	32	43	57	64	66	43	48	100
	Legislated	25	37	49	53	47	15	15	34
	Delegated	7	7	7	11	19	28	33	66
Directives	All	5	14	31	43	37	30	49	69
	Legislated	5	14	31	43	37	22	18	27
	Delegated	0	0	0	0	0	8	31	42
% Regulations		87%	75%	65%	60%	64%	59%	49%	59%
% Delegation	Regulations	21%	16%	13%	17%	28%	65%	69%	66%
	Directives	0%	0%	0%	0%	0%	28%	63%	61%
	Combined	18%	12%	8%	10%	18%	50%	66%	64%

Table A4.7 DC: 08 Competition

		1970–4	1975–9	1980–4	1985–9	1990–4	1995–9	2000–4	2005–7
Regulations	All	15	22	20	25	28	18	19	29
	Legislated	6	8	8	10	10	0	0	4
	Delegated	9	14	12	16	18	18	18	25
Directives	All	0	0	3	3	3	3	1	1
	Legislated	0	0	2	1	1	0	0	0
	Delegated	0	0	1	2	2	3	1	1
% Regulations		100%	98%	88%	88%	91%	87%	95%	97%
% Delegation	Regulations	0%	0%	0%	62%	65%	100%	98%	87%
	Directives		0%	38%	71%	79%	100%	100%	100%
	Combined	0%	0%	4%	63%	66%	100%	98%	88%

Table A4.8 DC: 09 Taxation

		1970–4	1975–9	1980–4	1985–9	1990–4	1995–9	2000–4	2005–7
Regulations	All	0	1	1	1	4	10	10	19
	Legislated	0	0	0	0	0	3	1	4
	Delegated	0	1	1	1	3	7	9	15
Directives	All	12	22	38	51	41	13	15	21
	Legislated	12	22	38	51	39	11	13	19
	Delegated	0	0	0	0	2	2	2	2
% Regulations		0%	3%	2%	2%	8%	43%	40%	47%
% Delegation	Regulations		100%	100%	100%	89%	73%	88%	80%
	Directives	0%	0%	0%	1%	5%	15%	14%	11%
	Combined	0%	3%	2%	3%	12%	40%	43%	43%

Table A4.9 DC: 11 External Relations

		1970–4	1975–9	1980–4	1985–9	1990–4	1995–9	2000–4	2005–7
Regulations	All	58	181	441	504	488	421	548	709
	Legislated	48	158	333	363	319	226	223	275
	Delegated	10	23	109	140	170	195	325	434
Directives	All	3	3	3	4	2	0	1	1
	Legislated	3	3	3	4	2	0	1	1
	Delegated	0	0	0	0	0	0	0	0
% Regulations		94%	98%	99%	99%	100%	100%	100%	100%
% Delegation	Regulations	17%	13%	25%	28%	35%	46%	59%	61%
	Directives	0%	0%	0%	0%	0%	0%	0%	0%
	Combined	16%	13%	24%	28%	35%	46%	59%	61%

Table A4.10 DC: 13 Industrial Policy and Internal Market

		1970–4	1975–9	1980–4	1985–9	1990–4	1995–9	2000–4	2005–7
Regulations	All	0	5	24	4	7	29	55	118
	Legislated	0	4	7	3	4	11	10	25
	Delegated	0	1	17	0	3	19	44	92
Directives	All	62	176	297	422	409	291	365	448
	Legislated	61	159	236	309	248	60	50	73
	Delegated	1	17	61	113	161	232	314	375
% Regulations		0%	3%	7%	1%	2%	9%	13%	21%
% Delegation	Regulations	0%	17%	73%	6%	41%	64%	81%	78%
	Directives	2%	9%	20%	27%	39%	80%	86%	84%
	Combined	2%	10%	24%	27%	39%	78%	85%	83%

Table A4.11 DC: 15 Environment, Consumers, and Health Protection

		1970–4	1975–9	1980–4	1985–9	1990–4	1995–9	2000–4	2005–7
Regulations	All	0	0	5	17	35	88	215	342
	Legislated	0	0	3	10	13	12	24	38
	Delegated	0	0	2	8	23	75	191	304
Directives	All	4	26	60	114	117	69	87	121
	Legislated	4	23	53	97	93	32	35	51
	Delegated	0	3	6	17	24	37	52	69
% Regulations		0%	1%	7%	13%	23%	56%	71%	74%
% Delegation	Regulations		100%	35%	44%	64%	86%	89%	89%
	Directives	9%	11%	11%	15%	20%	54%	60%	57%
	Combined	9%	12%	12%	19%	30%	72%	81%	81%

Directives and regulations by author institution and legal basis

Table A5.1 Legal basis of the directives and regulations adopted by the Commission 1970–2006

DC:	CU	AG	FISH	SOC	REFS	TRANS	COMP	TAX	EXTER	IPIM	ECH	Total
Legal basis in treaty article	23	36	2	9	3	0	21	0	0	13	2	109
ALL	4935	16525	1959	125	42	173	85	22	3832	747	511	28956
% total based in treaty article	0.5%	0.2%	0.1%	7.2%	7.1%	0.0%	24.7%	0.0%	0.0%	1.7%	0.4%	0.4%

Table A5.2 Directives and regulations adopted by the Council 1970–2006

DC:	CU	AG	FISH	SOC	REFS	TRANS	COMP	TAX	EXTER	IPIM	ECH	Total
Legal basis in regulation or directive	92	1631	594	10	4	5	0	4	836	23	12	3211
ALL	2875	3828	991	162	105	190	48	125	2416	482	300	11522
% based in regulation or directive	3.2%	42.6%	59.9%	6.2%	3.8%	2.6%	0.0%	3.2%	34.6%	4.8%	4.0%	27.9%

References

Akerlof, G. A. (1970). The Market for 'Lemons': Quality Uncertainty and the Market Mechanism. *The Quarterly Journal of Economics, 84*(3), 488–500.

Alfé, M. and Christiansen, T. (2009). Institutional Tensions in the Evolution of the Comitology System. In T. Christiansen, J. M. Oettel, and B. Vaccari (eds), *21st Century Comitology. Implementing Committees in the Enlarged European Union*. Maastricht: Institut Européen d'Administration Publique, 49–70.

Arrow, K. J. (1985). The Economics of Agency. In J. W. Pratt and R. J. Zeckhauser (eds), *Principals and Agents: The Structure of Business*. Cambridge, MA: Harvard Business School Press.

Bacharach, S. B. and Lawler, E. J. (1981). *Bargaining: Power, Tactics, and Outcomes*. San Francisco, CA: Jossey-Bass.

Bergström, C. F. (2005). *Comitology. Delegation of Powers in the European Union and the Committee System*. Oxford: Oxford University Press.

Bergström, C. F. and Héritier, A. (2007). Institutional Rule Five: Controlling the Implementation Powers of the Commission (Comitology). In A. Héritier (ed.), *Explaining Institutional Choice in Europe*. Cambridge: Cambridge University Press.

Bergström, C. F., Farrell, H., and Héritier, A. (2007). Legislate or Delegate? Bargaining over Implementation and Legislative Authority in the EU. *West European Politics, 30*(2), 338–66.

Blom-Hansen, J. (2011a). The EU Comitology System: Taking Stock Before the New Lisbon Regime. *Journal of European Public Policy, 18*(4), 607–17.

Blom-Hansen, J. (2011b). Interests, Instruments and Institutional Preferences in the EU Comitology System: The 2006 Comitology Reform. *European Law Journal, 17*(3), 344–65.

Blom-Hansen, J. and Brandsma, G. J. (2009). The EU Comitology System. *Journal of Common Market Studies, 47*(4), 719–40.

Bogdandy von, A., Arndt, F., and Bast, J. (2004). European Law – Cases, Legal Instruments in EU Law and their Reform: A Systematic Approach on an Empirical Basis, *Yearbook of European Law, 23*(1), 57–89, 91–136.

Bradley, K. S. C. (1997). The European Parliament and Comitology: On the Road to Nowhere? *European Law Journal, 3*(3), 230–54.

Brandsma, G. J. and Blom-Hansen, J. (2011). The post-Lisbon battle over comitology: another round of the politic of structural choice. EUI Working Papers SPS 2011/03.

References

Brousseau, E. and Glachant, J.-M. (eds) (2008). New Institutional Economics. Cambridge University Press.

Burns, C. (2005). The European Parliament: The EU's Environmental Champion? In A. Jordan (ed.), *Environmental Policy in the European Union*. London: Earthscan.

Carey, J. M. (2000). Parchment, Equilibria, and Institutions. *Comparative Political Studies, 33*(6–7), 735–61.

Checkel, J. T. (2001a). Constructing European Institutions. In M. Aspinwall and G. Schneider (eds), *The Rules of Integration: Institutionalist Approaches to the Study of Europe*. Manchester: Manchester University Press.

Checkel, J. T. (2001b). From Meta- to Substantive Theory? Social Constructivism and the Study of Europe. *European Union Politics, 2*(2), 219–26.

Checkel, J. T. (2001c). Why Comply? Social Learning and European Identity Change. *International Organization, 55*(3), 553–88.

Christiansen, T. and Kirchner, E. (eds) (2000). *Committee Governance in the European Union*. Manchester University Press.

Christiansen T. and Vaccari, B. (2009). The 2006 Comitology Reform: Problem Solved or Conflict Postponed? In T. Christiansen, J. M. Oettel, and B. Vaccari (eds), *21st Century Comitology. Implementing Committees in the Enlarged European Union*. Maastricht: Institut Européen d'Administration Publique, 333–52.

Christiansen, T., Oettel, J. M., and Vaccari, B. (eds) (2009). *21st Century Comitology. Implementing Committees in the Enlarged European Union*. Maastricht: Institut Européen d'Administration Publique.

Cooley, A. and Spruyt, H. (2007). *Contracting States. Sovereign Transfers in International Relations*. Princeton, NJ and Oxford: Princeton University Press.

Corbett, R. (1998). *The European Parliament's Role in Closer EU Integration*. London: Macmillan.

Davis, C. L. (2004). International Institutions and Issue Linkage: Building Support for Agricultural Trade Liberalization. *American Political Science Review, 98*(1), 153–69.

Dehousse, R. (2003). Comitology: Who Watches the Watchmen? *Journal of European Public Policy, 10*, 798–813.

Deringer, A. (1962). Rapport du 5 Octobre 1962 ait an nom du comite des presidents sur le 5e rapport general sur l'active de la communaunte europeenne (rapporteur Arvad Deringer). European Parliament 5.10.1962, EP Document 74/1962.

Elster, J. (1989a). *The Cement of Society*. Cambridge: Cambridge University Press.

Elster, J. (1989b). *Nuts and Bolts for the Social Sciences*. Cambridge: Cambridge University Press.

Epstein, D. and O'Halloran, S. (1999). *Delegating Powers: A Transaction Cost Politics Approach to Policy Making under Separate Powers*. New York: Cambridge University Press.

Epstein, D. and O'Halloran, S. (2006). Trends in Substantive and Descriptive Minority Representation, 1974–2000. In D. Epstein, R. de la Garza, S. O'Halloran, and R. Pildes (eds), *The Future of the Voting Rights Act*. New York: Russell Sage Foundation Press.

Farrell, H. and Héritier, A. (2003). Formal and Informal Institutions under Codecision: Continuous Constitution Building in Europe. *Governance, 16*(4), 577–600.

Farrell, H., and Héritier, A. (2004). Interorganizational Cooperation and Intraorganizational Power: Early Agreements under Codecision and Their Impact on the Parliament and the Council. *Comparative Political Studies 37*(4), 1184–212.

Farrell, H. and Héritier, A. (2006). Codecision and institutional change. *RSCAS Working Papers, 2006/41*. Florence: European University Institute.

Fearon, J. D. (1998). Bargaining, Enforcement, and International Cooperation. *International Organization, 52*(2), 269–305.

Fiorina, M. (1982). Legislative Choice of Regulatory Forms: Legal Process or Administrative Process. *Public Choice, 39*, 33–66.

Fiorina, M. (1986). Legislator Uncertainty, Legislative Control, and the Delegation of Legislative Power. *Journal of Law, Economics, and Organization, 2*, 33–51.

Franchino, F. (2000). Control of the Commission Executive Functions: Uncertainty, Conflict and Decision Rules. *European Union Politics, 1*, 63–92.

Franchino, F. (2001). Delegation and Constraints in the National Execution of the EC Policies: A Longitudinal and Qualitative Analysis. *West European Politics, 24*(4), 169–92.

Franchino, F. (2002). Efficiency or Credibility? Testing the Two Logics of Delegation to the European Commission. *Journal of European Public Policy, 9*(5), 677–94.

Franchino, F. (2004). Delegating Powers in the European Community. *British Journal of Political Science, 34*, 449–76.

Franchino, F. (2007). *The Powers of the Union: Delegation in the EU*. Cambridge: Cambridge University Press.

Frieden, J. (1999). Actors and Preferences in International Relations. In D. A. Lake and R. Powell (eds), *Strategic Interaction in International Relations*. Princeton University Press.

Gehring, T. (1999). Bargaining, Arguing and Functional Differentiation of Decision-Making—The Role of Committees in Environmental Process Regulation. In C. Joerges and E. Vos (eds), *EU Committees: Social Regulation, Law and Politics*. Oxford: Hart, 195–217.

Gilardi, F. (2005). The Institutional Foundations of Regulatory Capitalism. The Diffusion of Independent Regulatory Agencies in Western Europe. *Annals of the American Academy of Social and Political Sciences, 598*(1), 84–101.

Golub, J. (1999). In the Shadow of the Vote. Decision-making in the European Community. *International Organization, 53*(4), 733–64.

Grossman, S. J. and Hart, O. D. (1986). The Costs and Benefits of Ownership: A Theory of Vertical Integration. *Journal of Political Economy, 94*, 691–719.

Guidi, M. (2010). Good or Bad Intentions? Explaining the Independence of Competition Authorities in the EU. Manuscript. Florence: European University Institute.

Habermas, J. (1987). *The Theory of Communicative Action*. Boston, MA: Beacon Press.

Heckathorn, D. D. and Maser, S. M. (1987). Bargaining and the Sources of Trans-action Costs: The Case of Government Regulation. *Journal of Law, Economics, and Organization, 3*, 69–98.

Helmke, G. and Levitsky, S. (2004). Informal Institutions and Comparative Polit-ics. *Perspectives on Politics, 2*(4), 725–40.

Héritier, A. (1997). Policy Making By Subterfuge: Interest Accommodation, Innovation and Substitute Democratic Legitimation in Europe – Perspectives from Distinct Policy Areas. *Journal of European Public Policy, 4*(2), 171–89.

Héritier, A. (1999). *Policy Making and Diversity in Europe: Escaping Deadlock.* Cam-bridge University Press.

Héritier, A. (2007). *Explaining Institutional Change in Europe.* Oxford and New York: Oxford University Press.

Héritier, A., Moury, C., Bischoff, C., and Bergström, C. F. (2009). Legislate or delegate: European Parliament and comitology. Unpublished manuscript.

Horn, M. J. and Shepsle, K. A. (1989). Commentary on 'Administrative Arrange-ments and the Political Control of Agencies': Administrative Process and Organizational Form as Legislative Responses to Agency Costs. *Virginia Law Review, 75*, 499–508.

Huber, J. D. and Shipan, C. R. (2002). *Deliberate Discretion? The Institutional Foundations of Bureaucratic Control.* New York: Cambridge University Press.

Joerges, C. and Neyer, J. (1997). From Intergovernmental Bargaining to Delibera-tive Political Processes: The Constitutionalisation of Comitology. *European Law Journal, 3*(3), 273–99.

Jozeau-Marigné Report, European Parliament, Doc. 115/68, Resolution 3.10.1968, Official Journal 1968, C 108/37.

Jupille, J. (2004). *Procedural Politics: Issues, Influence and Institutional Choice in the European Union.* New York: Cambridge University Press.

Karagiannis, Y. (2007). Economic theories and the science of inter-branch rela-tions. *RSCAS Working Papers*, 2007/04. Florence: European University Institute.

Knight, J. (1992). *Institutions and Social Conflict.* Cambridge: Cambridge Univer-sity Press.

Knight, J. (1995). Models, Interpretations, and Theories: Constructing Explan-ations of Institutional Emergence and Change. In J. Knight and I. Sened (eds), *Explaining Social Institutions.* Ann Arbor, MI: University of Michigan Press.

König, T., Luetger, B., and Dannwolf, T. (2006). Quantifying European Legislative Research: Using CELEX and PreLex in EU Legislative Studies. *European Union Politics, 7*(4), 553–74.

Koremenos, B., Lipson, K., and Snidal, D. (2001). The Rational Design of Inter-national Institutions. *International Organization, 55*, 761–99.

Krasner, S. D. (1991). Global Communication and National Power: Life on the Pareto Frontier. *World Politics, 43*(3), 336–66.

Laffont, J.-J. and Tirole, J. (1993). *A Theory of Incentives in Procurement and Regula-tion.* Cambridge, MA: MIT Press.

Lake, D. A. (1999). Global Governance, A Relational Contracting Approach. In A. Prakash and J. A. Hart (eds), *Globalization and Governance*. New York: Routledge.

Lake, D. A. and Powell, R. (1999a). International Relations: A Strategic-choice Approach. In D. A. Lake and R. Powell (eds), *Strategic Choice and International Relations*. Princeton, NJ: Princeton University Press.

Lake, D. A. and Powell, R. (1999b). *Strategic Choice and International Relations*. Princeton, NJ: Princeton University Press.

Lax, D. A. and Sebenius, J. K. (1986). *The Manager as Negotiator: Bargaining for Cooperation and Competitive Gain*. New York: Free Press.

Lenaerts, K. and Desomer, M. (2005). Towards a Hierarchy of Legal Acts in the European Union? Simplification of Legal Instruments and Procedures. *International Law Papers*, *11*(6), 744–65.

Lewis, J. (2003). Institutional Environments and Everyday EU Decision Making: Rationalist or Constructivist? *Comparative Political Studies*, *36*, 97–124.

Lewis, J. (2005). The Janus Face of Brussels: Socialization and Everyday Decision Making in the European Union. *International Organization, 59*(4), 937–71.

Lupia, A. and McCubbins, M. (2000). Representation or Abdication? How Citizens Use Institutions to Help Delegation Succeed. *European Journal of Political Research, 37*(3), 291–307.

McCubbins, M. D. (1985). The Legislative Design of Regulatory Structure. *American Journal of Political Science, 29*(4), 721–48.

McCubbins, M. D. and Schwartz, T. (1984). Congressional Oversight Overlooked: Police Patrols versus Fire Alarms. *American Journal of Political Science, 28*(1), 165–79.

McCubbins, M. D., Noll, R. G., and Weingast, B. R. (1987). Administrative Procedures as Instruments of Political Control. *Journal of Law, Economics, and Organisation, 3*(Fall), 243–77.

Majone, G. (1996). *Regulating Europe*. New York: Routledge.

March, J. and Olsen, J. (1989). *Rediscovering Institutions: The Organizational Basis of Politics*. New York: Free Press.

Maynard Smith, J. (1982). *Evolution and the Theory of Games*. Cambridge: Cambridge University Press.

Miller, G. J. (2005). The Political Evolution of Principal–Agent Models. *Annual Review of Political Science, 8*, 203–25.

Mitchell, R. B. and Keilbach, P. M. (2001). Situation Structure and Institutional Design: Reciprocity, Coercion, and Exchange. *International Organization, 55*(4), 891–917.

Moe, T. M. (1984). The New Economics of Institutions. *American Journal of Political Science, 28*(4), 739–77.

Moe, T. M. (1990). Political Institutions: The Neglected Side of the Story. *Journal of Law, Economics, and Organization, 6*(Special Issue), 213–61.

Moury, C. and Héritier, A. (2013). Shifting competences and changing preferences: the case of delegation to comitology. *Journal of European Public Policy, 20*(1).

References

Napel, S. and Widgrén, M. (2008). The European Commission—Appointment, Preferences, and Institutional Relations. *Public Choice, 137*(1), 21–41.

Nicoll, W. (1998). The Evolution of the Office of the Presidency. Paper presented at the conference 'The Presidency of the European Union', Dublin, 15/16 October 1998.

North, D. (1990). *Institutions, Institutional Change and Economic Performance*. Cambridge: Cambridge University Press.

Osborne M. J. and Rubinstein, A. (1990). *Bargaining and Markets,* San Diego, CA: Academic Press.

Pollack, M. A. (1997). Delegation Agency and Agenda Setting in the European Community. *International Organization, 51*(1), 99–135.

Pollack, M. A. (2003). *The Engines of European Integration: Delegation, Agency and Agenda-Setting in the EU*. New York: Oxford University Press.

Ponzano, P. (2009). Brèves considérations sur le rôle de la Commission européenne. *Revue du Droit de l'Union Européenne, 2,* 217–20.

Ponzano, P. (2010). *La nouvelle comitologie et les actes délégués*. Workshop of the Robert Schuman Centre for Advanced Studies, European University Institute, Florence, 11–12 February.

Puettner, U. (2003). Informal Circles of Ministers—A Way Out of the EU's Institutional Dilemmas? *European Law Journal, 9*(1), 109–24.

Puettner, U. (2004). Governing Informally: The Role of the Eurogroup. *Journal of European Public Policy, 11*(5), 854–70.

Putnam, R. D. (1988). Diplomacy and Domestic Politics: The Logic of Two-Level Games. *International Organization, 42*(3), 427–60.

Püettner, U. (2003). Informal Circles of Ministers: A way out of the EU's Institutional Dilemmas? *European Law Journal, 9*(1), 109–24.

Raiffa, H. (1982). *The Art and Science of Negotiation*. Cambridge, MA: Harvard University Press.

Rasmussen, A. (2007). Challenging the Commission's right of initiative. Conditions for institutional change and stability. *West European Politics, 30*(2), 244–64.

Riker, W. H. (1980). Implications from the Disequilibrium of Majority Rule for the Study of Institutions. *American Political Science Review, 74*(2), 432–46.

Risse, T. (2000). Let's Argue! Communicative Action in World Politics. *International Organization, 54*(1), 1–39.

Ross, S. (1973). The Economic Theory of Agency: The Principal's Problem. *American Economic Review, 63*(2), 134–9.

Sebenius, J. K. (1992). Challenging Conventional Explanations of International Cooperation: Negotiation Analysis and the Case of Epistemic Communities. *International Organization, 46*(1), 323–65.

Sened, I. (1991). Contemporary Theory of Institutions in Perspective. *Journal of Theoretical Politics, 3*(4), 379–402.

Snidal, D. (1996). Political Economy and International Institutions. *International Review of Law and Economics, 16*(1), 121–37.

Stacey, J. and Rittberger, B. (2003). Dynamics of Formal and Informal Institutional Change in the EU. *Journal of European Public Policy, 10*(6), 858–83.

Steunenberg, B., Koboldt, C., and Schmidtchen, D. (1996). Policymaking, comitology, and the balance of power in the European Union. *International Review of Law and Economics, 16*, 329–44.

Strom, K. (2000). Delegation and Accountability in Parliamentary Democracies. *European Journal of Political Research, 37*(3), 261–89.

Sugden, R. (1986). The Economics of Rights, Co-operation and Welfare. Oxford: Basil Blackwell.

Sverdrup, U. (2005). Implementation and European integration: A review essay. *ARENA Working Paper Series*, 25/2005 at http://www.arena.uio.no/publications/working-papers2005/papers/05_25.xml, accessed 26 October 2010.

Taylor, M. and Singleton, S. (1993). The Communal Resource: Transaction Costs and the Solution of Collective Action Problems. *Politics and Society, 21*, 195–214.

Thomson, R. and Torenvlied R. (2011). Information, commitment, and consensus: a comparison of three perspectives on delegation in the European Union. *British Journal of Political Science, 41*(1), 139–59.

Toeller, A. E. (1998). The 'Article 19 Committee': The Regulation of the Environmental Management and Audit Scheme. In M. P. C. M. Van Schendelen (ed.), *EU Committees as Influential Policymakers*. Aldershot: Ashgate.

Tsebelis, G. (1990). *Nested Games. Rational Choice in Comparative Politics*. Berkeley, CA: University of California Press.

Ullman-Margalit, E. (1978). Invisible Hand Explanations. *Synthese, 39*, 263–91.

Weale, A. (2000). Governing by committee: three principles of evaluation. In T. Christiansen and E. Kirchner, *Committee Governance in the European Union*. Manchester University Press.

Weale, A., Pridham, G., Cini, M., Konstadakopulos, D., Porter, M., and Flynn, B. (2000). *Environmental Governance in Europe*. Oxford: Oxford University Press.

Weber, M. (1958). *The City*. New York: Free Press.

Wessels, W. (1998). Comitology: Fusion in Action. Politico-Administrative Trends in the EU System. *Journal of European Public Policy, 5*, 209–34.